The Battle for "Charlie"

John J. Duffy

John J. Duffy

Published in the United States

ISBN-13: 978-1499683615
ISBN-10: 1499683618

Cover painting
"The War Years"
By Nguyen Cao Nguyen

John J. Duffy

The War Years

(Major Nguyen Cao Nguyen)

The temples are burning
In a land of milk and honey.
The women are beautiful
In a land without men.

The war years painted by an Artist
Nuyen Cao Nguyen is brilliant.
His strokes of paint tell a story,
A story of women and war.

This is a very large painting
Splashed with the beauty of the tropics
And the flames of a landscape afire.
All wars are terrible, we should remember.

DEDICATION

To the men and officers of the 11th Vietnamese Airborne Battalion who still hold the ground on "Charlie" and their Commander, Colonel Nguyen Dinh Bao, who was killed in action leading his beloved paratroopers.

To the gallant helicopter pilots who performed fearlessly in the battle and are all heroes.

To the Forward Air Controllers (FACs) who controlled the attack bombers and the B-52 boxes.

To the survivors of the battle for "Charlie" – the toughest paratroopers that I've had the honor to serve with in battle.

To LTC Le Van Me, the bravest officer I know and his equally gallant Operations Officer, Major Hai P. Doan.

Note: A "B-52 box" is three B-52s simultaneously releasing 108 bombs each (500 and 1,000 pound mix) for box destruction of approximately 1/2 by 1/3 kilometer.

John J. Duffy

ACKNOWLEDGMENTS

Carol von Raesfeld,
For her assistance with publishing this book

Dorothy Hardy
For the cover design

Charlie Witmer,
For photographing the cover painting

Michael Duffy
For editing assistance

Thomas Duffy
For editing assistance

Colonel Le Van Me,
For translating and editing assistance

John J. Duffy

FOREWORD

This is a poetry book with documentation for an upgrade to this nation's highest valor award, the Medal of Honor. The Distinguished Service Cross had been awarded previously for this action: The Battle for "Charlie."

With the discovery of a tape recording made by one of the helicopter rescue pilots, Dennis Watson, it became evident that there was additional documentation and there were new witnesses we could identify by name matched against "call signs."

The upgrade process began anew in 2012. The recommendation had previously been denied for lack of documentation and witnesses. The witness statements are the second section of this book.

An excerpt from the rescue tape is included as an Appendix. The biographies of the participants' forty-plus years after this battle are included. These soldiers all went on to enjoy successful careers in the military and in civilian careers. I am honored to have been part of their story. I owe them my life and the lives of my fellow paratroopers that they saved. They were each and every one of them heroes in a far-off war. They have all been honored by their nation.

John J. Duffy

TABLE OF CONTENTS

SECTION I: POETRY

The War Years

TABLE OF CONTENTS *(cont.)*

Distinguished Service Cross

The End of the Vietnam War

TABLE OF CONTENTS *(cont.)*

John J. Duffy

TABLE OF CONTENTS *(cont.)*

SECTION III

BIOGRAPHIES

General Fred C. Weyand
LTC Pete Kama
LTC Me Van Le
Major Terry A. Griswold
Major Hai P. Doan
Colonel William S. Reeder, Jr.
CW4 Daniel E. Jones
Major Forest B. Snyder, Jr.
LTC James M. Gibbs
CW4 Dennis Watson
Captain Nam Nhat Phan

APPENDIX
Transcript

SECTION I

POETRY

AUTHOR'S NOTE

In the Spring of 1972, the North Vietnamese Army launched a major offensive with fourteen Infantry Divisions and twenty-six separate Regiments supported by long-range Russian artillery and 1,200 armored vehicles and tanks. The enemy force was 150,000 strong. In the Central Highlands, three Divisions, plus separate regiments were in the attack. I was the lone American Advisor to the Vietnamese 11th Paratrooper Battalion. The paratroopers were tasked to block the critical mountain pass to the Kontum region.

Of the 471 men committed, I came out after two weeks of intense battle with 36 survivors, most of whom had been wounded.

Note: Translation and poetic license help tell the story of the battle for Fire Base "Charlie."

John J. Duffy

Battle Call

Know the soldier's call,
Hear the order clear,
Into combat now!
Kill or find and end.

Call forth the courage.
Be prepared to die.
Remember life's gifts—
Then you can survive.

Battle Plan

North Vietnamese Army (NVA)
Central Highlands Commander briefing
Commanding General 320th (NVA) Division

We move southwest from Cambodia,
Down the old French Highway.
It has been rebuilt for heavy trucks.
It is camouflaged and not known about.

Cross over the mountains at Hill 1015.
There is a pass, it will be blocked,
Most likely by a Paratrooper Battalion.
Smash through them, advance to Route 14.

Route 14 will take you to Kontum.
There should be little or no resistance.
They have committed their Reserves
Believing they could hold us in the mountains.

Once Kontum is taken, reorganize.
The next move will be toward the Coast.
Our Forces have already secured the Coast.
A link-up will divide South Vietnam.

A simple plan, do not fail to execute.
This has taken four years to organize.
You have the privilege of leading our soldiers.
Execute rapidly, that is key to success.

Battle Deployment
**(General Lich and Colonel Peter Kama
Brigade Commander and Senior Advisor)**

"The NVA will attempt to break through.
The pass at Hill 1015 is their best choice.
We must place our best Commander there.
This battle will be decisive for Kontum.

The NVA rebuilt the old French road last year.
It will allow them to reinforce and resupply.
They will attack on this high finger ridge.
It'll lead right into our best defensive zone.

The 11th Battalion deploys here,
Colonel Bao commands.
He is fearless and a very determined leader.
His paratroopers respect his judgment.
He has some of my best officers in the Brigade.

The Advisor is experienced, on his third tour.
He is big and tough and very combat savvy.
The only problem, he has no back-up.
He told me, 'Not to worry, I'll handle it.'

OK. The best battalion for the toughest mission,
This will be a fight to the death for Firebase Charlie.
What is the Advisor, Major Duffy's call sign?
Sir, he is designated "Dusty Cyanide."

"Perhaps a bad omen for the NVA."

Clarification notes re Battle Deployment

1. "NVA" refers to "North Vietnamese Army"–the enemy.
2. Hill 1015 is the height in meters of the mountain above the pass.
3. Kontum was decisive to the defense of the Central Highlands in South Vietnam.
4. Advisor Team normal complement: Two officers and two non-commissioned officers.
5. Call Signs: Names designating the leaders on the battlefield.

Combat Assault Briefing

It is a four ship Landing Zone.
Recon Platoon will go in first.
Have an Artillery Observer with them,
Just in case we need fire support.

Flight time is fifteen minutes.
Each platoon will require four ships.
Split headquarter personnel amongst them.
Commanders go in on the lead ship.

The LZ is expected to be cold, but be prepared.
The NVA are moving from Cambodia.
Hill 1015 is the best crossing point.
They must get through the mountains.

The insertion should require two hours.
Get in, off load and prepare defenses.
Expect an attack, be prepared.
I will follow Recon, second flight lead.

**Are there any questions? If not,
Check your men, check your commo.
Prepare your reverse loading order.
We will do battle, fight light a paratrooper.**

Courage
(Doctor To Pham Lieu,
Cross of Gallantry with Palm)

The Doc has been shot at.
Oh, Lord! He has his gun out,
Sighting, aiming, and shooting
At a cannon with a forty-five.

He is hit and down,
But not for long,
Back up again,
Sighting, aiming, shooting.

Trying to knock out a cannon
With his forty-five.
God, isn't he ridiculous?
But he has courage.

Soup

White chicken, red comb,
Running back and forth
In the midst of battle,
Knowing not where to go.

Soldiers, fighting and dying all around,
Damn chicken doesn't know where to go.
What the hell, does it matter?
Tonight it will be in someone's soup.

Be Brave

Too many incoming,
The battle has begun,
Explosions of steel flash.
This fight will kill many.

Be brave my comrades.
What else can we do?
There is no escape.
Kill or die is our fate.

The Commander's Order

The NVA have us surrounded.
They hold the mountain tops.
They have positioned their guns
To shoot down the helicopters.

It is here we must do battle.
It is here we must bleed them.
Do not let them take our positions,
This battle is to the end.

Tell the paratroopers to fight bravely.
Tell them to aim all of their bullets,
For we will not have a resupply.
Dig in deep and prepare for combat.

Any trooper not ready to fight,
I want him off the mountain.
I'll not have him die with us.
I'll not have him share in our glory.

Ungiven Command

Why have they lingered?
I do not know.
They should have retreated.
Now they will die.

Do they not know better?
What is the reason?
They are caught between us
And certain death.

The dark would have hidden them,
Allowing them to escape,
Who didn't give the command
For them to withdraw?

Let them eat breakfast,
For it will be their last.
The bunkers they are in
Will soon be their tombs.

A Tribute to Love
(Le Van Me letter to his wife)

This may be my last letter for awhile.
The situation is approaching critical.
The Colonel is doing all that is possible.
The NVA will push forward and we will battle.

I will soon fight in a ferocious battle.
The Commander and the paratroopers are ready.
Perhaps all will not return from this battle.
That is the fate of soldiers serving their country.

My thoughts will always encompass you.
My heart will always belong to you.
My strength is a tribute to your love.
Our children are a testament to our love.

Do not worry when you hear the reports of battle.
I am ready and I know how to survive in combat.
I will come back home to you, my precious love.
I will battle the dragons and return to your arms.

Bird's Eye Six
(NVA spotter team leader "call sign")

Overlooking the "Charlie" bunkers,
An NVA artillery spotter team observes all.
The job is to destroy the bunkers
And to kill the Commanders of "Charlie."

"The Commander just went into his bunker.
The Advisor is already is in his bunker.
It is time to execute our fire plan.
They will never know what hit them.

"Give me the radio and watch the bunkers."
"Red Fire, this is Bird's Eye Six, over.
Birds Eye Six, this is Red Fire, over.
Fire mission, three bunkers on Charlie.

Twenty kilometers away, the gun rolled on tracks
To its firing point outside a mountain tunnel.
"From Charlie One Register, ninety meters south,
"First one round, I'll adjust from impact."

The 130-millimeter shell impacted.
"From impact, adjust forty meters east.
Direct hit. Fire three rounds for effect.
Bunker destroyed, shift target north sixty meters."

"Gunner, one round—on target, three for effect.
Gunner, next target, shift thirty meters west,
Fire one round—on target, three for effect.
Report: three bunkers destroyed, Six out."

John J. Duffy

Direct Hit

The dust is choking.
The others are dead.
The radio still talks:
I must be alive.

The loud ringing noise,
Will it never stop?
I am half buried
In someone else's grave.

My bunker is destroyed.
I crawl over the bodies.
All are dead or dying.
I must kill that gun!

Colonel Nguyen Dinh Bao (right)

"KIA"

**Shells are exploding,
Always digging deeper.
Three direct hits impact.
The Commander looks bad.**

**KIA: Killed in Action.
Wrapped in a poncho,
He'll lie in that hole
That was dug for him.**

The Commander's Burial
(Colonel Nguyen Dinh Bao)

We wrapped him in a poncho,
Even his dismembered legs.
He had known that he was dying
And he spoke his last words.

"Tell my wife I loved her true.
Tell my children to remember me.
Tell my paratroopers to never surrender.
You, my officers, one final salute."

He lays in a shallow grave alone,
No bugles, no farewell rifle salute,
Only a few shovels of red earth.
His grave is marked with his helmet.

He fought bravely until the end.
He fought against heavy odds.
He has fought his last battle.
With his glory, we leave him.

The New Commander
(Colonel Le Van Me)

He lost his friend and Commander.
The Executive Officer takes command.
His burden is great, his duties heavy,
But he is strong, fearless, and experienced.

His staff and commanders receive orders.
"We will hold 'Charlie,' it is critical.
If the NVA break through, Kontum will fall.
There are no Reserves left, only us paratroopers."

"Duffy, can you take out the NVA guns?"
"If I have air support and someone covering me,
I will eliminate every gun that shoots.
That is what I can do. I will not fail you."

"Major Hai, see that Duffy is covered.
Pick the best man we have, no failures."
All agreed that "Charlie" must be held.
This will be a battle to the last man.

Killing the Guns

"Major Duffy is on the perimeter.
He is being targeted by the NVA.
He's in the open, he'll never last.
He is too big a target. They want him."

"He is changing location every few minutes.
He targets the guns, knocks one out
And then he is running to a new spot."
"Everywhere he goes, the enemy targets."

"He has taken out the Spotter Team.
He has taken out four AA guns.
He is going after the 130 artillery."
"Them blowing his bunker up got his attention."

Planes Above

It must be me
They're shooting at.
That's the third time
I've been blown up.

It's the radio
They have spotted.
They know I'm talking
To the planes above.

I have to keep moving,
Hoping they don't see me.
Keep moving and talking
To the planes above.

They are in low and hot
Dropping big bombs and nape,
Making the enemy shudder
And convulse, before his end.

Death's Breath

**Death's moment is near,
I can feel its flame.
Soon it will be here,
It seems strange no more.**

The Machine Gunner

They are coming forward.
"Hold the trenches!"
"Set up that weapon!"
"Don't fall back!"

The bastard is still pulling back,
Shooting between his legs.
Fear and reality flash into his eyes.
He turns and faces him enemy.

Machine gun down and bolt back.
Firing...Killing.
Rat-a-tat-tat...
Look at them die.

John J. Duffy

Rocket Ridge

Blown up, wounded, deafened,
But never fearful,
The godless enemy came forward,
Knowing well how to die.

The battle raged back and forth.
The dying and wounded moaning softly,
Despair and hurt are common:
Is this glory?

Attack and counter-attack,
To and fro this battle rages.
Brave soldiers dying on both sides,
Only the righteous know why.

Delayed Fuse

I counted the moments by,
I knew I was to die.
The shell which landed close
Did not explode this time.

I had seen my end:
Knowing I was dead.
Time seemed to tick by,
Each moment eternal.

John J. Duffy

[Arrows indicate bullet holes.]

Dance of Death
(Panther 36-Bill Reeder)
(Panther 13-Dan Jones)

"Panther Lead, this is Dusty Cyanide."
"Dusty Cyanide, this is Panther Lead."
"I have multiple targets for you,
All fifty-one caliber machine guns."

Panther Lead was given locations,
Advised that the guns were all hot
And that the gunners were eager.
He flew off into the sun to set up.

I watched him come out of the sun.
He was targeting the high gun first.
He flew straight into the gun,
Blazing away with his mini-gun.

John J. Duffy

From the hilltop, the gun opened fire.
The green and red tracers crossing,
Then the Cobra fired his rockets,
The gunner and gun vanished in the explosion.

Four times I watched this performance.
It was a dance of death between gunners.
The North Vietnamese lost this fight,
Four gun crews destroyed, four guns taken out.

"Dusty Cyanide, this is Panther Lead.
Be advised, running low on fuel,
And I'm bingo on ordinance.
Enjoyed the hunt, do call on us again."

Hell's Moment

It's an inferno:
Smoke, dust and flame,
Shattering explosions
Shred a moment's stillness.

Soldiers running fast,
Away from the flashes,
Trying to escape,
Afraid of death.

The smell of battle,
Choking smoke and dust,
Life's last moments
Caught in an explosion.

Night's darkness will come
In but a short time.
Perhaps some will live,
Fleeing into the shadows.

Retreat!

They keep coming forward.
Twice we have stopped them
With a murderous fire.
They still keep coming.

The troopers are pulling back,
Out of ammunition and frightened.
It is just the deadly planes
Holding the enemy wave back.

Only a few more minutes
And darkness will be here.
They will attack before then.
That will be the end.

Retreat and escape
Before it's too late.
The orders are given.
We prepare to break out.

"We Are a Team"
**(Cobra pilots: Bill Reeder, Dan Jones,
Forrest Snyder, Dennis Trigg, Owen McFarland,
Sam Scott, Robert Gamber, David Messa,
Ron Lewis (WIA), and Captain McDonald)**

The paratroopers were pulling back,
Major Hai Doan was leading them.
They were spent, out of ammunition,
Many wounded, all hungry and thirsty.

"I'll cover the withdrawal with air."
The Cobra gunships were flying above us.
I'll use them to disrupt the enemy.
I'll work them close to cover the break-out.

The new Commander, Colonel Le Van Me:
"I'm staying with you, you need cover.
We are a team, we have fought together
And if need be, we will die together."

"Panther Lead, this is Dusty Cyanide.
The enemy is closing on us from our west.
They are advancing in the trenches.
Hit them hard, break up their attack."

The Cobras swooped down with guns blazing.
"Adjust fire! Drop three meters!"
Blow them away. Work it close.
The Cobras worked with deadly precision.

The explosions were hot and blinding.
The shrapnel shredded the enemy.
Hit in the chest, Colonel Le Van Me staggered.
I was peppered with hot fragments of steel.

The Cobras stopped them. That was close.
"Let's go, Colonel, it's time to get away."
Bleeding from wounds, but joyful,
We get up and run away from death.

[Note: This poem and "Break Out" which follows cover the same event in the battle with different emphasis.]

Break Out

The NVA keep pushing forward.
The ammo situation is critical.
The paratroopers are pulling back.
Our time is fast running out.

The decisions are made quick:
Break out to the northeast,
I'll use gunships to cover
While we disengage and run.

Colonel Le Van Me is at my side.
He is my back-up and my cover.
We work as a team in battle
And this may be our last battle.

I had been working the gunships.
Ever closer the enemy advanced.
They were ten meters distance
When "Cougar" Lead blasted them away.

The Panther gunships were now in.
They broke the next enemy attack.
The NVA reform and push forward.
Panther flight blasts them away again.

"Panther Lead, this is Dusty Cyanide.
You have broken the enemy attack.
We are leaving Firebase Charlie now.
Stop them from following us!"

The Panther gunships wreaked havoc.
We moved away from the battle,
Escaping from a certain death,
Bloodied, but not yet broken.

Archlight
(B-52 cell, three aircraft)

"Covey Nine Nine, this is Dusty Cyanide, over."
"Dusty Cyanide, this is Covey nine nine, over."
"Covey, Dusty, we are moving off "Charlie."
I have a target request for you, over."

"Dusty, go ahead, pass your request."
"Covey, request Archlight strike on 'Charlie.'
Target, two battalions of NVA troops in the open.
Request strike be executed as soon as possible."

"Roger, Dusty, Covey, stand by one!"
"Dusty, that is an affirmative.
An Archlight is being diverted to 'Charlie.'
You need five hundred meters distance, over."

"Covey, this is Dusty moving northeast,
Give me fifteen minutes to get distance, over."
"Dusty, Bingo plus twenty minutes 'til drop.
I'll advise pre-release of the bombs, out."

"Dusty, this is Covey, one minute warning."
"Roger, Covey, we are in defilade, over."
"Dusty, bombs released, impact ninety seconds,
Hang onto your steel pots and open your mouths!"

"Covey, you rattled us good with that load.
Report" 'Charlie' obliterated and smoking.
Casualties, no bomb damage report possible.
Covey, thanks, we are moving northeast, out."

[Note: Each B-52 carried a mix of *500* and *1,000* pound bombs, 108 total, dropped for 324 bomb strike with three B-52s in a box.]

Check Fire
(Night Withdrawal)

"Incoming. Everyone, get down!"
"That's 105 fire from our own batteries.
Who the hell gave the clearance to fire?
They're killing our own paratroopers."

"Brigade, Dusty Cyanide calling, over."
"Dusty Cyanide, this is Brigade Three."
""Brigade 105 artillery is hitting us.
Do you have a fire mission working?"

""Dusty, that is 113 Company fire mission."
"Brigade, impact is killing my paratroopers.
Check fire! Check fire! Immediately!"
"Dusty, Check fire in place, confirmed."

"Brigade, this is Dusty Cyanide,
I have three KIA and seven WIA.
Who authorized this fire mission?"
"Dusty, 113 Company requested this mission."

"Brigade, did you clear this fire mission?"
"Dusty, affirmative, I'll plot you on my map."
"Brigade, do not authorize fire missions.
Check with me before you approve, over."

**"Dusty, roger that, I will clear all fire missions.
We'll post your progress on the map board.
Is there anything else we can do for you?"
"Aside from blowing your brains out, no."**

"Dusty Cyanide Out!

New Dawn

My eyes have been blinded.
I am stumbling in the dark.
I cannot see anything,
Slipping down a jungle path.

I am in water now.
Damn! It's over my head.
Let me drink deep
While I have the chance.

I'll tread my way out of here,
Up onto a jungle path
And walk myself
Away from here.

I've been moving many hours,
Guided by a young trooper's hand.
Once buried by the panicked herd
When friendlies bombarded us.

That hill was straight up.
Made it on my hands and knees.
But coming down now,
Sliding fast on my ass.

Stepped on the Doc then.
I still can't see worth a damn,
But wait! I see trees and the sky.
A new dawn is here.

Ambush

The *swoosh* of the mortar,
The *rat-a-tat-tat* of the machine gun,
Fear dominates the green soldiers.
Panic herds them into the killing zone.

Lord, how easily they die,
Their lips silently moving.
Appeals of the young to mother and God
As blood bubbles from between their lips.

Escape

The young green troopers panic,
Running away from the sound of fire.
Down toward the stream and death
Where the killing guns draw blood.

Break away! The path of least resistance.
Move fast! Don't get caught in the panic.
Move quick! Go! Go! Keep moving!
The veterans are still with you.

It takes time to kill the bunched herd,
Time needed to break out,
Shooting when necessary,
But always moving quickly.

Snipers on the hilltops,
Trying to channelize movement.
Disregard! Disregard!
Their aim is high.

Far enough now.
Stop! Everyone quiet!
Security move out!
Radio operating...contact.

The first chopper in takes fire.
The enemy is close and to the south.
Return fire! Gunships in on them!
The firing slackens off.

John J. Duffy

Two more lifts out.
Gunfire picking up again.
Moving, placing distance.
Last ship in, hanging on.

Bullets lacing the air,
Chopper gaining height.
Cordite and tension fill the air.
We've made it, we're out!

But damn!
Two men hit:
One screaming,
The other dying.

Crew Chief's End
(Crew Chief Dallas Nihsen, KIA)
(Major Hai Doan, WIA)
(Pilots: Major "Mike" Gibbs (Silver Star)
(and WO Dennis Watson (Distinguished Flying Cross)

Three lifts loaded and off.
It's out bird coming in fast.
The gunfire is picking up.
The enemy knows we're escaping.

On approach the pilot takes heavy gunfire.
He circles and is coming back in.
Touchdown, enemy fire riddles the ship.
We're running fast and scramble aboard.

We're lifting off and flying,
Flying away from a jungle battle.
Major Hai's foot is shattered
By a 51-caliber bullet.

The Crew Chief is hit and hanging,
Held in the aircraft by his tether.
He's unconscious and needs help.
I climb to his side of the aircraft.

I drag him back into the helicopter.
He's hit just about his chicken plate,
A clean wound that needs patching.
I apply my bandage to his wound.

John J. Duffy

I turn him over and find the exit wound.
It's big and it's still bubbling.
I'll quick patch and stop the bleeding.
The bubbles stop before I'm finished.

[Note: Dallas Nihsen, the gunner, and Major Hai Doan, the Operations Officer, were taken to the Pleiku Medical Station.]

The Operations Officer
(Major Hai Doan, WIA)
(Cross of Gallantry w/ Palm* and
Bronze Star w/Valor device)

It had been the fiercest of battles.
The Battalion Commander had been killed,
Company Commanders lost leading their men,
The Executive Officer and the Advisor wounded.

Two weeks holding the enemy waves back.
Incoming artillery a routine happening.
Surrounded by a North Vietnamese Regiment.
Heavy machine guns above us on the high ground.

Finally, the break-out into a pitch black jungle.
Friendly fire inadvertently killing paratroopers.
The check fire and the morning ambush,
Breaking through the "kill zone" to escape.

The advisor leads us to an opening,
Enough room for a helicopter pick up.
He forms a perimeter and redistributes ammo.
On his radio, he calls for an extraction.

The NVA have pursued us to our location.
We engage in battle for more than an hour.
The lift ships arrive and begin the extraction.
Three lifts out, only the command group remains.

John J. Duffy

We await the last lift ship's arrival.
The enemy wants to capture our group.
The enemy shouts our names to surrender.
We answer with gunfire and Cobra attacks.

I'm the last to board except for the Advisor.
He jumps on the strut. I'm hit and falling.
I'm falling to my death, I know I am dead.
Hands grab me and haul me back into the aircraft.

My leg is shattered by an enemy bullet.
It hurts. I hear myself screaming.
I know with so much hurt and pain
I must be alive. Life is still mine.

Warrior's Gun
(CAR-15, Serial #906557)

The helicopter flew north to Brigade.
It had been a desperate battle.
We had held the enemy back.
We had stopped them for two weeks.

The battalion had fought well.
The new commander, Colonel Le Van Me
Was a determined, fearless warrior.
I was proud to have been his advisor.

My CAR had been given to me
By another fierce warrior.
I had promised to pass it on
To a warrior worthy of the gun.

At the time, this gun had status.
I handed it to Le Van Me and said,
"Only a warrior has rights to this gun."
His eyes teared up just a bit.

He held the gun as a new friend.
"I will honor this gun as a warrior.
I will fight for my beloved country
With courage and the gun of a hero."

Colonel Le Van Me

Notes re Warrior's Gun

Note 1: Captain James Butler, a decorated "Green Beret" hero presented this gun to Major Duffy.

Note 2: Colonel Le Van Me is one of his country's most decorated officers: National Order of Vietnam, Knight; Army Distinguished Service Cross; seven Gallantry Crosses with Palm; six Gallantry Crosses with Gold, Silver, or Bronze Star; three wound medals; and, American medals: Silver Star; Bronze Star with Valor Device.

Letter of Hope

Colonel Le Van Me's letter was delivered
By a Captain from Headquarters staff.
He gave Sen, Le Me's wife, the letter
And he awaited her instructions.

Sen opened and slowly read the letter,
Her young children playing in the garden.
Tears slowly ran down her cheeks.
She thanked the Captain for his courtesy.

Sen read and re-read the letter again,
It was her reassurance while waiting.
She heard all the reports of battle:
Fierce fighting reported on "Firebase Charlie."

She trusted and believed her husband.
She so wanted him to come back to her,
To return to their three small children
And to be the father of his family.

The reports from the North Vietnamese
Claimed that they had killed or captured
All of the paratroopers that had fought
On "Firebase Charlie," including Colonel Le Me.

John J. Duffy

She held his letter close at night.
Teardrops stained the pages of the letter.
He had promised to return to her.
The letter was her last hope.

She heard his knock on her door.
She gasped and ran to the door.
Her man had returned as he promised.
He laughed at her tears and kissed her.

Colonel Nguyen Dinh Bao

The Commander's Family
(Colonel Nguyen Dinh Bao Memorial Service)

Can you picture the scene?
Incense burning, banners hung, casket draped.
The moans and the weeping blend,
Sorrow hangs in the atmosphere.

The Commander's comrades gathered
To offer their last salute.
The young widow, strong at first,
Bur soon sorrow overcomes her.

It's not the smoke which tears my eyes,
Although I have lit seven joss sticks.
The words are spoken for all to hear.
Now, it is I who must say the last.

I will say the truth and how he died.
"He died leading the paratroopers he loved."
He died fighting for the freedom he cherished."
He died a hero of his country!"

DISTINGUISHED SERVICE CROSS

The author was honored with the award of the "Distinguished Service Cross" for actions with the 11th Airborne Battalion. The citation states:

DISTINGUISHED SERVICE CROSS

"For extraordinary heroism in connection with military operations involving conflict with an armed hostile force in the Republic of Vietnam:

Major Duffy distinguished himself while serving as the Senior Advisor, 11th Airborne Battalion, Airborne Division, Army of the Republic of Vietnam at Fire Support Base Charlie, Kontum Province, Republic of Vietnam during the period 14 and 15 April 1972.

Beginning with the morning of the 14th and continuing for a period of approximately twenty-four hours, Major Duffy repeatedly made heroic contributions to the defense of the fire base. When attempts at resupplying the base were still being considered, Major Duffy exposed himself to the effects of the continuous bombardment the base experienced as he targeted anti-aircraft weapons and adjusted airstrikes on them.

When the resupply attempts were abandoned, Major Duffy moved about the base, continuing to expose himself to the enemy fire, treating and finding shelter for wounded Vietnamese defenders. During the early evening initial ground assault, Major Duffy ignored the massive small arms fire as he adjusted gunships and artillery on the advancing enemy formations. When the enemy finally gained control of a portion of the base and advanced to within ten meters of his position, Major Duffy was the last man off the base, remaining behind to adjust the covering gunships until the last possible moment.

After the Battalion Commander was wounded, Major Duffy assumed command and led the formation through the night. Finally, when the battalion was ambushed and the unwounded soldiers abandoned their wounded comrades, Major Duffy remained with the wounded and eventually was able to arrange for their extraction. Major Duffy's conspicuous gallantry in action was in keeping with the highest traditions of the military service and reflects great credit upon himself, his unit, and the United States Army."

* * * * *

In the aftermath of the battle for Firebase "Charlie," an award-winning book was written about the battle, *The Red Flames of Summer*" by Nam Nhat Phan.

A song was composed by Tran Thien Thanh, "The Ones Who Stayed at Charlie." This is a weak effort at interpretation of that song. Translators: Le Van Me and John J. Duffy.

The bodies of the fallen were left where they fell in battle. This song is still sung by Vietnamese to lament their fallen warriors.

The Ones Who Stayed At "Charlie"
Nguoi O lai Charlie

Oh you! The ones who stayed at "Charlie."
Oh you! The ones who died in battle.
Yes, you are the nation's newest heroes.
You were the bravest of the brave.
We mourn your passing with sorrow.

Yes, you, the ones who stayed at "Charlie."
Oh yes, you are now with heaven's angels.
Oh yes, you are a warrior returning home.
Only now we cry our tears of sorrow.

The day you departed, you said, "Goodbye."
You left your home one last time.
Your footfalls are no longer heard.
Your absence is felt by all of us.
We mourn you with white headbands.
Your lonely children cry in sadness.
Your widow dreams of you at night.

John J. Duffy

We know the names of Dak To, Kre, Snoul,
windy Khe Sanh, and the moonlit Laos.
"Charlie" is not a Vietnamese name place.
Oh you, you stayed at "Charlie"
Just stayed at "Charlie."
"Charlie," we didn't know that name before.

You, you, will you miss the monsoon rains?
You, you, will you remember the colors of the forest?
Oh! Have you arrived at your destination?

Forever! We will love you forever!
My warrior who will not return,
I say one more time, one more time,
I say goodbye to you on "Charlie."
I say one more time, one more time,
I say goodbye to you on "Charlie."

I will remember you forever
As I talk to my warrior gone to heaven.

Requiem For Those On Charlie
(KIA, April 1972)

You can walk up the mountain to "Charlie."
You are required to take a guide with you.
"Charlie" has become a tourist attraction,
A battle site from a long ago war.

Two hundred meters from "Charlie's" top,
You see the signs that indicate danger.
There are unexploded bombs above you,
Too many to clear in a safe manner.

It's just as well that this is so
As the soldiers from both sides rest above.
Some were hastily buried in shallow graves,
Others strewn about from the fallen bombs.

These men gave their lives in battle.
Both sides, the South Vietnamese paratroopers
And the North Vietnamese Army soldiers
Fought and died in the battle for "Charlie."

The stories of struggle, combat, heroes, and death,
They were told in poetry, books, and a famous song.
The song grieves for all who died in the war.
It is sung around the world, teardrops lament the fallen.

John J. Duffy

Salute the fallen Vietnamese of a war now long past.
Remember a husband, your father, or a brother.
They were men of courage who fought to their death.
Remember the face, whisper the name of a hero.

Heroic Engagement By Vietnamese Paratroopers on the Southern Front. "The Battle for An Loc."

The Red Beret
(Battle of An Loc)
April 20, 1972

The enemy, reinforced during the night.
They were intent on destroying the battalion.
The airborne troops of the 5th Battalion
Dug in deeper, preparing their defenses.

The green tracers came in from our front.
The mortar rounds impacted among us.
The smoke and haze of the battle intensified.
Our red tracers cut into the attack formation.

The battalion was engaged in a death struggle.
No matter how many NVA we managed to kill,
More came out of the rubber trees of An Loc.
We were about to be overrun by the NVA.

The orders were given during a lull in the battle:
"51st Company, hold the line—all others disengage!"
The 51st Commander repositioned his paratroopers.
He now had to hold the enemy as long as possible.

The paratroopers knew this was their last assignment.
First, the Commander removed his combat helmet.
He replaced it on his head with his "red beret."
The rest of the paratroopers followed his example.

The NVA came out of the rubber trees firing.
They crossed the defensive road and we killed them.
New attacking NVA formations followed behind them
Until it was kill or die in the trenches of An Loc.

In the smoke and dust, the noise of battle was heard.
51st Company no longer existed. They were all dead.
This fight allowed their fellow paratroopers to escape.
They died fighting, wearing their "red beret."

Stopping the Enemy on
The Northern Front.
"The Battle for Quang Tri"

Blasting Tanks
(Task Force Le Van Me)
June 22, 1972
(My Chanh River, south side)

**The battalion was part of a holding force.
The command was bringing in reinforcements
Before attacking across the My Chanh River.
And driving north to push the NVA from Quang Tri.**

**Twelve tanks and six armored track vehicles,
Two more companies of paratroopers were attached
I now commanded a powerful spearhead unit.
I was tasked to defend Hue, hold the NVA at the river.**

Patrols reported enemy tank movement at the river.
The NVA had a crossing point and crossed at night.
The first probing attack came in the morning.
It was only three tanks. We destroyed them.

I repositioned my armor, awaiting their next attack.
It came at dawn, two dozen tanks with infantry.
I first called in artillery fire on the approaching tanks.
Next, it was attack aircraft that targeted them.

Most still rolled forward, at 300 meters,
I gave the order. "Fire!" My tanks blasted them.
My anti-tank guns fired, my machine guns opened up.
All killed the enemy—blasting, gunning, and shooting.

The dust cleared. Only burning NVA tanks remained.
The battalion had killed twenty-four tanks.
Our gunners slaughtered a battalion of NVA infantry.
The remnants of the enemy retreated across the river.

We had lost two tanks plus a dozen killed.
Another twenty had been wounded, few seriously.
I placed artillery fire on the retreating NVA force.
That would be the last time they crossed the river.

The Bridge No One Crossed
(My Chanh River)
(19 kms south of Quang Tri)
(LTC Peter Kama, Senior Advisor)

**I was the Senior Advisor to a
Vietnamese Airborne Brigade.
We were advancing to recapture Quang Tri
From the North Vietnamese Army.**

**The "Easter Offensive of 1972"
Proved to be the fiercest battles of the war:
Three separate fronts...150,000 enemy in the attack.
South Vietnam was fighting for its survival.**

**Two major battles in the south had been won.
Now we needed to recapture Quang Tri.
The NVA had attacked south along the coast.
They had come very close to capturing Hue.**

**I had fought in the "Kontum Battle."
Now we must defeat their main thrust.
We were moving north toward Quang Tri.
We were tasked to destroy the NVA.**

John J. Duffy

We crossed a river and we saw death.
The bridge had been destroyed by the NVA.
Refugees fleeing war were stopped at the river.
The NVA systematically killed them with gunfire.

The killing had been done several days before.
The vehicles were burned out, the bodies mummified.
A macabre view of war, death, and destruction.
Even tough soldiers can cry at horror and brutality.

Stunned, I wandered through the death scene.
I picked up a little shoe with a foot in it.
I could not find the rest of the child's body.
Everything had been destroyed and bypassed.

A line of destroyed vehicles five kilometers long,
25,000 dead, innocents fleeing the war.
Only the vultures and rats visited here.
"What the hell is this war about?" I voiced.

No one answered. The dead do not talk.
Inhumanity does not respond. No press coverage.
The voices were silenced, bodies decaying in the sun.
I wept for a child, a parent, a grandmother.

I wept for mankind.

The Valley of the Shadow of Death
(LTC Peter Kama)

The enemy had mounted an attack:
Fourteen Divisions on three fronts.
My job was to stop the northern thrust,
Four Divisions strong, moving straight toward us.

I was with an elite Airborne Brigade.
I advised and coordinated firepower.
The Brigade Commander relied on me.
It was my job to bring in the ordnance.

The enemy's vanguard was moving south,
Two Regiments reinforced with tanks.
There were in a valley two miles from us,
Preparing their units for the assault.

I needed to engage this enemy force
Before they could close in and crush us.
We could not persevere against armor.
I needed bombers to destroy them.

I contacted the General on my radio:
"I need flights of B-52 bombers,
I need all you can get, right now."
Two flights, six aircraft were diverted.

In two hours, they would arrive.
I had a table set up with a white cloth.
I took out two bottles of cognac and glasses,
I had saved them for a special occasion.

Before noon, on the Fourth of July, 1972,
Just south of the Demilitarized Zone,
I invited the airborne command and staff
To join me in a celebration toast.

On schedule, at noon, the bombers arrived.
They released their loads of destruction,
Six hundred bombs of whistling death.
Where the enemy was, fire and smoke arose.

I lifted my glass of cognac and toasted,
"Happy 4th of July. Happy Independence Day."
My Vietnamese Commander offered his toast,
"To victory, freedom, and independence."

Note: With Colonel Le Van Me's Task Force stopping the North Vietnamese Army's tanks at the My Chanh River and General Lich's Brigade (LTC Peter Kama, Senior Advisor) destroying 119 reinforcement tanks, the NVA push in the north was halted.

The mop up campaign north to Quang Tri was a pursuit in force by Marine/Airborne units.

The North Vietnamese soldiers would tattoo on their arms, "Born in the North to Die in the South" and so the final failure of "The Easter Offensive of 1972" was concluded.

The End of the Vietnam War

Vietnam, Spring of '75

**Khe Sanh, Quang Tri
Kontum, Pleiku,
The provinces fall...
Where I have fought.**

**Four years fighting,
Watching friends die,
Awaiting my moment,
Learning not to smile.**

**Now it seems in vain,
As the provinces fall,
Only Tay Ninh remains
Of where of I have fought.**

**The rest soon fall.
New flags wave high
Over old citadels.
A new order marches.**

John J. Duffy

Escape From Vietnam

Colonel Le Van Me
**(Awarded his nation's highest award for valor,
The Cross of Gallantry with Palm seven times.**

Le Van Me became an officer.
Learning all that was needed
To survive and lead soldiers
In the war that ravaged Vietnam.

He found his love and married.
Soon he began a family.
He had a son and two daughters,
Hoping he would live to see them grow up.

He fought in the battles,
Surviving when others died.
In time, he commanded the best,
Paratroopers wearing the red beret.

His deeds became legend.
He was the commander who fought
And never suffered defeat,
Always standing while others fell.

But the day Saigon fell,
He had to make his choice.
Flight and freedom he sought,
Risking all on the open seas.

Escape From Vietnam

The new masters know terror:
The terror of retribution,
The terror of hopelessness,
The terror of life in fear.

Colonel Le Van Me must flee.
His family is his hope
For he no longer commands.
His Vietnam is in defeat.

He commandeers a boat.
His family is loaded aboard,
Refugees on the high seas,
Fleeing the storm of terror.

No water, no food, only hope,
Hope that they will escape,
Hope for freedom without chains,
Hope for a new beginning.

The boat is open-decked.
It soon runs out of fuel.
The seas swamp the bottom
With foul, salty water.

John J. Duffy

Their plight is desperate.
The children are thirsty and tired.
The nights are cold and very wet.
All are full of hopeless despair.

Six days without rescue—
Until off the Philippines,
A warship picks them up
And hope's flame burns again.

The New Americans

It's time to begin anew.
It's time to begin the future.
"We will not linger here."
"We'll go anywhere you say."

With three very young children
And a very pregnant wife,
Colonel Le Van Me departs
On the "Freedom Bird" of hope.

Thousands have fled Vietnam.
The camp is in Arkansas,
At an old Army base.
They receive a "Welcome Kit."

The baby is soon born.
Le Van Me looks at the mountains.
They are east, on the horizon.
They are the Ozark Mountains.

He says, "My son is American,
He will be named as such."
To honor my new country,
"We'll call him Ozark Le."

John J. Duffy

Fifteen Years of Torture and Retribution

(Post Vietnam War, 1975-1990)

John J. Duffy

The Re-education Camps

With defeat, my world vanished.
I was no longer a being in self.
I was an enemy of the new State.
I was to be re-indoctrinated to obey.

I reported as ordered to the police.
I was to be re-educated into society.
The education camp was in the jungle
Where I was transported without trial.

I must have been stupid or stubborn
For I refused to bow to the Communists.
I refused to worship Chairman Ho Chi Minh.
I refused my education on socialism.

After a year of stubborn refusal,
My captors determined I needed reform.
I was placed in wooden stocks.
I was isolated underground to rehabilitate.

For nine years I was allowed to reform,
Nine years alone in my wooden stocks,
Nine years kept alive while underground,
I never changed my views. I never bent.

Three more years of re-education in the camp.
I worked as ordered by my captors.
In time, I must have seemed reformed.
One day, after thirteen years, I was released.

Thereafter, I escaped their jurisdiction.
I escaped their indoctrination of fear.
I escaped to a life of being a free man.
I escaped Vietnam, Communists, and subjugation.

I walk in freedom. I earn my bread.
I believe in hope and aspiration.
I relish each day of my freedom.
I'm free from repression, torture, and Communism.

My Name is Nam Nhat Phan!

[Note: Nam Nhat Phan is a celebrated author, lecturer, and talk show host. His heroic resistance while in captivity is acknowledged by all.

John J. Duffy

Exodus Epilogue

Almost forty years have gone by
Since the fall of Saigon.
The images are of defeat,
Frozen in a photograph.

Desperate people gaining entry
To the Embassy grounds
And flight from the rooftop—
One helicopter at a time.

The pilots crashing their planes
Near the evacuation ships,
Hoping for rescue and freedom,
Again the fear of retribution.

The victorious enemy tanks
Crashing through the Palace gates,
Raising the flag of the North
Over the citizens of the South.

The exodus never stopped.
The flight was always desperate.
The Vietnamese freedom lovers
Sought escape to other lands.

More than three million did flee,
In boats over open seas.
Some were set upon by pirates,
Others by the bureaucrats of freedom.

But, many achieved an escape
And as a foreigner in a new land,
They worked as opportunity allowed.
These were the refugees of Vietnam.

Now, many years later,
Settled in their new countries,
Established, and many successful,
They look toward the future.

The future is their children,
Now educated and employed.
They are the new society,
Blending some old with the new.

The Land of Opportunity
(Refugee children)

Our families escaped terror:
The terror of defeat in war,
The terror of torture and prison,
The terror of retribution forever.

The culture of America is ours.
The culture of Vietnam is heritage.
We are a blend of past and future.
We are hungry for the opportunity.

We owe our parents our freedom.
They made the dangerous crossing.
We owe them obligations to do our best.
We need to study, work, and achieve.

Only in America can we sing, "Freedom!"
Freedom to be part of the American culture.
Freedom to be part of the American Dream.
Freedom to be in "The Land of Opportunity."

SECTION II

MEDAL OF HONOR RECOMMENDATION STATEMENTS

General Fred C. Weyand
LTC Peter Kama
LTC Me Van Le
Major Terry A. Griswold
Major Hai P. Doan
Colonel William S. Reeder, Jr.
CW4 Daniel E. Jones
Major Forest B. Snyder, Jr.
LTC James M. Gibbs
CW4 Dennis Watson
Captain Nam Nhat Phan

John J. Duffy

FRED C. WEYAND
SUBMISSION LETTER

July 7, 1998

Honorable Daniel K. Inouye
Prince Kuhio Federal Building
300 Ala Moana Blvd., Suite 7-212
Honolulu, Hawaii 96850

Dear Senator Inouye:

This correspondence is to support the efforts of Peter Kama in his quest to recognize the valor in combat of the highest order for John Duffy, a courageous American soldier, who served under Major Kama during some of the toughest fighting in the Vietnam War.

Peter served as my Aide-de-Camp in Vietnam from November 1970 to December 1971. He volunteered to return to combat duty advising the 2nd Vietnamese Airborne Brigade. This was during the final period of the exodus for our ground troops (January 1972-July 1972) and many support units as well. The Vietnamese were in the offense responding to heavy losses in the Northern and Western regions.

Many advisors were alone with their counterparts and as happened with the 442nd Regimental Combat Team many years before, there were many valorous actions that went unrecorded or were not accorded the official recognition that they deserved.

Hopefully this submission will be favorably received and reviewed.
Sincerely,
(signed)
Fred C. Weyand
General, U.S. Army, Retired

S-T-A-T-E-M-E-N-T
July 27, 2012

As Senior Advisor to the 2nd Airborne Brigade during the Easter Offensive of 1972, I was directly senior to Major John J Duffy, the Senior Advisor to the 11th Airborne Battalion. His unit was posted to my Brigade on April 1, 1972.

This recommendation for the Medal of Honor covers multiple acts of conspicuous gallantry and intrepidity in action at the risk of his life above and beyond the call of duty during the period April 12, 1972 through April 15, 1972.

The 11th Airborne Battalion was combat assaulted on April 2, 1972 onto Rocket Ridge to protect the supply route of Highway 14 in the Central Highlands of Vietnam. This position was designated Firebase Charlie. Major Duffy was the only advisor to be committed with the battalion as there was a shortage of personnel and the normal complement is four advisors, but not less than two. He was capable and confident that, pending additional advisor complement, he could handle the responsibilities.

PRELUDE: The battalion had contact with the enemy from the first day. On April 3 an NVA (North Vietnamese Army) unit, estimated at battalion size, attempted to dislodge the friendly force from its positions and was repulsed. Enemy forces continued the engagement with artillery directed into friendly positions and both sides suffered casualties. The battle continued to develop with enemy probes, indirect fire, and rocket fire. Major Duffy was instrumental in holding the enemy at bay with TACAIR and Cobra gunship support, plus his counterparts employed VNAF (Vietnamese Air Force) and artillery. On April 4, another NVA battalion was repulsed. The NVA employed 105mm and 130mm artillery, plus they began to emplace AA 51MG's on the high ground ringing the pass that FSB "Charlie" was blocking during the next week.

RECOMMENDATION PERIOD: Beginning the morning of April 12, 1972 with the enemy making Company-sized attacks supported by indirect fire, Major Duffy exposed himself continuously to enemy fire in order to employ air assets against the attacking enemy formations, their AA .51MG, mortar and artillery positions.

Prior to noon on April 12, three of the four command bunkers were destroyed by direct hits from 130mm artillery within a ten minute period. The Battalion Commander was mortally wounded and died. Major Duffy received a second wound and he was the only one to survive from his bunker. When queued as to being medically evacuated, he refused as he was needed to protect the battalion. He became mobile, working air strikes and repulsing the enemy until nightfall, whereupon, he passed out from a concussion with his radio receiver still in hand.

During the night, the enemy attacked, attempting to overrun a company size unit. Major Duffy came on the radio and directed Spectre (C-123 artillery platform) through a small hole in the clouds, ringing the defenses with lethal fire and repulsing the enemy attack.

Major Duffy was wounded again on the afternoon of the 13th while working air strikes. He continued to roam the perimeter, always a target for the enemy as they knew that he, with his radio antenna, was directing the air strikes. The NVA AA .51MG in the late afternoon shot down two VNAF A1E's over FSB

"Charlie." Major Duffy advised the LZ (Landing Zone) was untenable as it was ringed by approximately ten AA .51MG's, all above the LZ. The effective closing of the LZ prevented medical evacuations, resupply and reinforcements. The unit was limited in its ability to perform its mission.

On April 14, Major Duffy continued to expose himself to enemy fire as he directed essential air strikes. He was wounded again early in the morning.

All afternoon on April 14, the enemy pounded FSB "Charlie" with direct and indirect fire (over 700 artillery incoming were counted). Major Duffy continually changing position, working air strikes against enemy gun positions, concentrating on eliminating the artillery and AA .51MGs. During the battle, Major Duffy employed 144 sorties against the NVA. His counterpart employed artillery and 71 sorties of VNAF support. The estimate losses to the enemy were 1250 KBA (Killed By Air), one 130mm artillery piece, one to three 105mm artillery pieces, five AA .51MGs, one Recoilless Rifle, two mortars plus 93 secondary explosions observed.

At 1645 hours on April 14, the southwest perimeter of "Charlie" was overrun by an estimated two NVA battalion force. Major Duffy redirected air strikes in progress to support the friendly element. The NVA continued to push forward. Friendly forces counter-attacked three times. VNAF and TACAIR supported the counter-attacks. Major Duffy and the new Battalion Commander, Major Le Van Me, were in the forefront directing the battle, they were a team.

Out of ammunition, the NVA still pushing forward, the decision was made to break out, perform a night withdrawal and regroup in the morning. Major Duffy volunteered to cover the withdrawal, an extremely valorous act as the enemy was numerous and determined. Major Le stayed at his side while the rest of the battalion withdrew. Major Duffy's radio and the Cobra gunships were their only defense. Major Duffy adjusted fire in "3 meter" increments, the enemy was advancing in the trench lines. The Cobra gunships would sweep down and kill them. One gun run, when the enemy was within ten meters of Major Duffy and Major Le, was made at "extreme danger close" parameters. Both Major Duffy and Major Le Van Me were wounded, they broke contact, running for their lives. Major Duffy continued to direct Cobras while on the run, preventing the pursuit from engaging. He also requested a B-52 strike (3 B-52s in a cell) on the abandoned position from a FAC (Forward Air Controller).

The command group rallied 400 meters from "Charlie," exhausted, but alive. They regrouped, Major Duffy was given command of the battalion as Major Le had a sucking chest wound and was disabled. Major Duffy gave orders for another company below them to rendezvous with them at first light and organized the night march.

The B-52 cell, diverted enroute to another target, dropped on "Charlie" twenty minutes after the withdrawal. The command group was rattled and shaken by the explosions on "Charlie." The survivors began their night march. During the night, friendly artillery fire hit the battalion (3 KIA, 7 WIA), Major Duffy "checked fire" and gave precise instructions on location, direction moving, and clearance required to Brigade "Watch Officer."

Major Duffy had suffered temporary flash blindness during the withdrawal from "Charlie." At first light on April 15, after covering 10-11 kilometers, the battalion was waiting to link-up with 113 Company and treating the wounded. Major Duffy returned command to Major Le. It became apparent that link-up would not occur as the enemy was between the two elements.

Major Le requested helicopter evacuation from Brigade for the 167 paratroopers remaining. Brigade had no air assets and advised Major Le to fight his way out. The Commander gave the march order and the unit was ambushed at that moment with NVA mortar and machine gun fire initiating. Many of the soldiers panicked and ran.

Major Duffy gathered many wounded and the intact command group, consulted with his counterpart, and they determined to break out. Major Duffy led the break out through the kill zone and approximately one kilometer distance established a defensive position near a workable Landing Zone. He contacted "Covey 555" (Forward Air Controller) on his emergency radio, "declared an emergency," and requested TACAIR, gunships and four lift ships for 37 paratroopers. The enemy had pursued the Command Group, were calling them and Major Duffy by name "to surrender or die". Major Duffy employed air assets to attack the NVA. This fight was fought for over an hour when four lift ships with Cobra guns came up on guard frequency, ready to extract. They requested Major Duffy board first (Americans had evacuation priority). He refused, advised he would be the "last man out."

The first lift ship took enemy fire. Major Duffy employed air assets to destroy the enemy machine gun position. Number 2 and 3 lift received little or no enemy fire. With the enemy in close pursuit, the Command Group ran to board Lift 4 ship. Major Duffy brought up the rear, covering with his CAR- 15 and directing the Cobras fire at the enemy on his survival radio. The ship was being riddled as they climbed aboard. Captain Hai Doan was hit in the foot and fell out. Major Duffy caught him as he fell and threw him aboard as they lifted off. Major Le gave first aid to Captain Hai. Major Duffy, seeing a door gunner outside the aircraft in lift off, held on by a tether, hauled him back in. He patched a chest wound, turned the door gunner over and began patching the exit wound when the gunner died in his arms.

CITATION: During the period April 12-15, 1972, at Fire Support Base "Charlie," Major John J. Duffy had been wounded five times during the battle, he refused medical evacuation two times, exposed himself continuously to enemy fire directed at him for four days. Directing air and gunship support, he stopped the enemy from over-running the battalion, destroyed numerous enemy, their guns, and their ammunition. On the night withdrawal, he volunteered to be the rear guard, stopped the enemy once again at extremely close quarters and destroyed the abandoned "Charlie" position after the withdrawal. He assumed command of the battalion in a difficult night withdrawal. After a friendly fire incident, he "check fired" friendly fire. Major Duffy successfully led the battalion and returned command to the Vietnamese as appropriate.

After the remnants of the battalion had been ambushed, he gathered many wounded and the Command Group. He led the break out through the kill zone, located a Landing Zone, established a defensive perimeter, and coordinated a rescue package. Waiting on rescue, he fought off enemy pursuit forces for over an hour. On extraction, he refused to board the aircraft until all the Vietnamese were evacuated first. On lift off of the last helicopter, under fire, he was last to board and caught a wounded officer falling from the aircraft, thus saved his life. After boarding the aircraft, he attempted to save the life of a wounded door gunner who died in Major Duffy's arms.

EFFECTIVENESS OF ACTIONS: Major Duffy implemented "danger close" tactical employment of B-52 boxes within the 300 meter parameter strike zone as the enemy were hugging his unit at the 300 meter range. This tactical employment, I passed on to General Weyand, who was the Commander, Military Advisor Command, directing the "Easter Offensive" battles. He forthwith employed this doctrine change. The "Battle of Kontum" was a close fought battle against a large NVA force supported by artillery and tanks. (estimate 35,000).

Major Duffy's actions contributed to the victory in the follow-on battle in the Central Highlands. Major Duffy delayed the enemy for over a week as they had to regroup after losses suffered and ammunition depleted, giving time to reinforce to the Commander. His "danger close" tactics with B-52's were utilized and proved critical in destroying the enemy. The Coastal Plains had been captured by the NVA and a defeat in Kontum would have linked up enemy forces cutting South Vietnam in half. This would have demoralized the people of South Vietnam significantly. I recommend Major John J. Duffy for this nation's highest award for valor, the Medal of Honor for conspicuous gallantry and intrepidity in battle at the risk of his life above and beyond the call of duty.

Peter Kama
LTC U.S. Army
(retired)
notarized

John J. Duffy

EYEWITNESS STATEMENT

Me Van Le LTC, Army of the Republic of Vietnam
Last active duty position: Airborne Division Operations Officer,
G-3, 1975
Position during statement: Executive Officer and Commanding Officer, 11th Airborne Battalion

Current Residence: San Jose, CA 95136
Occupation: Retired Senior Engineering Manager, Samsung Information Systems,
Citizen: USA

Major Duffy was the senior advisor to the 11th Airborne Battalion. We had previously campaigned with the battalion in the Tay Ninh Area of Operations and during the Cambodian Incursion, before the Easter Offensive campaign. However, during the two-week campaign at Kontum in April of 1972, Major Duffy was the finest combat officer that I have ever met.

The 11th Battalion of the Airborne Division of the Republic of Vietnam (470 men and officers) combat assaulted on April 2, 1972 into Fire Support Base Charlie in an effort to stem or contain the offensive actions of the North Vietnamese 320th Division. We initially placed our units in the best defensive positions possible, taking maximum advantage of the terrain and the anticipated direction of attack by the North Vietnamese Army (NVA). Our position was located on Rocket Ridge north of Kontum and was designated Fire Support Base (FSB)

Charlie. The initial contacts were with probing enemy forces and battalion also received considerable enemy artillery, mortar, recoilless rifle, and rocket fire.

On April 11, 1972, while our battalion command post was under heavy incoming 130mm enemy artillery, Major Duffy bravely left the safety of our bunker to direct the friendly air strikes, effectively enough to knock out one of the 130mm artillery pieces. He also directed friendly aircraft onto the massing enemy infantry positions. Risking his life and exposing himself to direct airstrikes was an extreme act of bravery.

On April 12. 1972, three of our four command bunkers took direct 130mm artillery hits within a few minutes of each other. LTC Bao, our Airborne Battalion commander, was mortally wounded. I assumed command of the battalion after he died. My bunker and Major Duffy's bunker both were destroyed.

During this entire engagement, even as he was the only one to survive from his bunker, Major Duffy appeared to be fearless, he calmly moved around the perimeter and directed airstrikes and automatic weapons fire on the approaching NVA Infantry to protect the battalion. He knew without his direction, critical American air support would not be available. He directed the aircraft and friendly artillery onto the NVA AA .51MGs, knocking out four of them in order for us to get our last resupply of ammunition, water and rations. He even refused medical evacuation, insisting that he had to protect the battalion. His courageous actions saved our ability to continue to fight by getting us the needed supplies.

In the early hours of the 13th, the NVA attacked one of our company positions, Major

Duffy, who passed out from a concussion with his radio in hand was awoken. He directed a Spectre C-123 gun platform fires onto the attacking NVA force, killing and disrupting their night attack. He stayed awake the rest of the night directing flare ship support. On the 13th, I continued to coordinate fires with Major Duffy, taking out enemy targets between us. We targeted our artillery, Vietnamese Air Force strike aircraft, both U.S. Air Force and U.S. Army attack aircraft and B-52 strikes against the NVA. The coordination was very effective and the enemy suffered heavy casualties. Both Major Duffy and I continually exposed ourselves in order to effectively direct fire on the enemy positions. We both suffered wounds, but these were not serious.

On April 14, 1972, our situation became extremely critical. FSB Charlie was ringed by .51 caliber AA machine guns, denying us any further resupply. With the ammunition running out, I ordered a break out from FSB Charlie. Major Duffy volunteered to cover the withdrawal with gunships and I stayed with him at this critical maneuver. During this battle of the rear guard, both of us were wounded as Major Duffy was forced to work the gunships ever closer. On the last enemy assault, the NVA were within a few meters of our position. Only his fire disrupted the attack. His efforts were instrumental in inflicting heavy casualties on the enemy and in saving the battalion during this phase of the withdrawal. Major Duffy and myself were the last two to leave the perimeter. As we broke contact, Major Duffy directed B-52 strikes on our former positions and the positions of the North Vietnamese.

I had sustained a sucking chest wound and I was incapacitated and Major Duffy temporarily assumed command of the battalion and led us out of the danger zone. Major Duffy then ordered Company 113 to link up with the remainder of the battalion at first light, where we could reorganize and redistribute ammo and conduct a successful retrograde operation.

On the morning of April 15, 1972, Major Duffy returned command of the battalion to me and briefed me before daylight on the actions that he had taken during the night. At first light, I ordered a halt in order to reorganize and to await the link-up with Company 113. It was determined that Company 113 was unable to break out and link-up was not imminent. I gave the order for the Companies to move out, concerned that we had remained too long in one location.

As the surviving 170 paratroopers were moving from our night defensive positions, the NVA initiated a battalion size plus ambush with small arms, 60mm mortars and automatic weapons, Our unit was devastated and scattered. Major Duffy and I organized the Command Group and Major Duffy led the breakout through the killing zone, Leading the way through the jungle, ignoring enemy fire, he found an LZ (landing zone). Major Duffy quickly organized the defense of the LZ with the 36 men that were left from our battalion, and utilized his emergency radio, quickly established communications with a FAC (Forward Air Controller). He requested an immediate helicopter exfiltration and many covering air strikes.

The NVA were oblivious to tremendous losses that they were sustaining and continued to close in and placed effective fire on the first extraction helicopter. Major Duffy immediately placed suppressive fire on the enemy gunners who were in a stream bed. He worked two sets of A-Is and two sets of Cobras. The second and third lifts got out without taking as much fire. At this point, there were only five of us remaining on the ground, including Major Duffy who refused to leave before everyone was out safely. Even though Americans had priority in evacuations, Major Duffy advised he would be "the last man out." The NVA regrouped and stormed the Landing Zone. As we drove for the aircraft, my S-3 Captain Hai was hit in the foot and was knocked out of the aircraft. Major Duffy, who was standing on the skid directing airstrikes, reached out and caught him and threw him back into the helicopter. Major Duffy continued to ride the skid until we cleared the LZ. The aircraft took numerous hits and the left side door gunner was hit in the chest. Major Duffy immediately jumped in and grabbed him and began to perform mouth to mouth resuscitation as he applied pressure bandages. The young door gunner died in Major Duffy's arms.

We rode to the Medical Evacuation facility. Major Duffy had been wounded six times over the last three days.

Major Duffy was an expert. He was where we needed him. He routinely exposed himself to enemy fire. He was fearless and a real leader for the paratroopers. His fighting abilities, especially with the strike aircraft, was incredible. His unselfish devotion to his duty and the men he commanded not only saved the 11th Airborne Battalion, but also the destruction of two complete battalions of the NVA's 320th Division. His ability to coordinate and advise was paramount to the survival of the command. Though Major Duffy was wounded several times, he never flinched. He was the last to leave FSB Charlie, and he took command in the moment of need. He held the command together during a night withdrawal, and was the last man to get on a rescue helicopter. Major Duffy trusted the ARVN paratroopers and they trusted him. I personally thank Major Duffy for saving my life. Without him, I could not imagine how and what my life would be. As a counterpart and on behalf of all of my surviving paratroopers, I deeply thank him. He is my hero and I respect him as one of the greatest soldiers of all time. Major Duffy performed with distinct bravery, expert knowledge, and tenacious fighting abilities. He deserves this nation's highest decoration for valor.

August 1, 2012
Me Van Le

WITNESS STATEMENT

The following statement is made in support of the previous recommendation for the Medal of Honor submitted by Major Peter Kama for Major John J. Duffy, in 1972. At that time I was Major Kama's deputy, with my duty position as the Deputy Senior Advisor, 2nd Airborne Brigade, Vietnamese Airborne Division, Army of the Republic of Vietnam (ARVN). I was assigned to the Airborne Advisory Detachment, Team 162, Military Assistance Command Vietnam (MACV) 1971-72.

REFERENCE: OAK TO Map Sheet, 653811, series 7014.

BACKGROUND

In March, 1972, the 2nd Airborne Brigade (ARVN) was deployed to the area north of the city of Kontum in Vietnam's Central Highlands. This was in response to the North Vietnamese Army's (NVA) build up in Base Area 609, and along the major NVA supply route commonly referred to as the HO CHI MINH TRAIL. Ground combat had been light but consistent during the month of March. In my capacity as Deputy Senior Advisor, I was operations officer at the 2nd Brigade Tactical Operations Center (TOC), located at Vo Dinh. I was a witness, through communications with/and debriefing of Major Duffy. The following is the account of the actions of Major John J. Duffy, Senior Advisor, 11th Airborne Battalion during the period April 1972. This account is based on information from my notebooks, and my own personal knowledge of that battle for FSB Charlie.

SITUATION

The 11th Airborne Battalion had been relocated from Red Hat Hill near Long Binh to Vo Dinh. On 2 April 1971 the battalion conducted combat assault by helicopter onto Fire Support Base (FSB) Charlie (XD009108). The enemy situation around FSB Charlie was active with several .51cal. heavy machine guns active near the fire base. NVA recon teams and platoon size units had been conducting operations against FSB Charlie's defensive perimeters. From 3 April until 10 April 1972, the NVA continued to develop the tactical situation. On 11 April, FSB Charlie and the 11th Airborne Battalion received over three hundred rounds of 130mm artillery fire. US and ARVN intelligence sources warned of a full scale assault against the line of FSBs along the mountain spine commonly referred to as Rocket Ridge. Numerous intelligence reports were received reporting NVA forces moving into staging areas west of Rocket Ridge (VIA990100).

The Battle for Fire Support Base Charlie

At 0700 hours on 12 April, I relieved the night shift operations officer, and was immediately involved in supporting combat operations on and around FSB Charlie. According to the Staff Officer Journal (DA Form 1594) / radio log, Major Duffy reported at 0655 hours, heavy mortar, RPG, and automatic rifle fire from enemy probes. These probes had evolved into a full scale assault, and the enemy force was estimated to be a re-enforced NVA infantry battalion. NVA 105mm and 130mm artillery fire was supporting the attack, and at 0745 hours, Major Duffy reported that a position designated as Charlie One had been overrun by the NVA after several attempts. The US Air Force Forward Air Controller (FAC), call sign COVEY 580, was cleared to use airstrikes on/around FSB Charlie under the direction of Major Duffy. The FAC immediately began to vector U.S. Air Force airstrikes against the

NVA. At this time, my Vietnamese counterpart asked that I instruct Major Duffy to use caution and take cover because his battalion commander was concerned that Major Duffy was exposed to heavy and accurate enemy fire. The request was passed to Major Duffy.

At approximately 1100 hours, a replacement FAC, call sign COVEY 565 reported in, and control was passed to Major Duffy. At 1130 hours, radio contact with Major Duffy was lost. My Vietnamese counterpart reported that 3 of the 4 command group bunkers had been knocked out by the enemy artillery, and the battalion commander was seriously wounded. Radio contact was re-established at 1150 hours, and Major Duffy reported the death of the battalion commander. Major Duffy assisted the executive officer in re-establishing control and continued to call in airstrikes. He provided instructions to Cobra gunships, call sign PANTHER, and COUGAR, and directed the supporting gunships against targets along the battalion perimeter. At 1600 hours, Major Duffy's bunker was destroyed by a direct hit from enemy 130mm artillery fire. Communications with Major Duffy was against lost.

Major Duffy re-established contact after moving to the alternate battalion command post. He and the new battalion commander (the former XO) had been wounded in the artillery strike. The Vietnamese operations officer reported that Major Duffy had sustained head wounds. When asked if medical evacuation was required, Major Duffy refused and informed us that the fire base was surrounded by approximately 8 anti-aircraft .51cal. HMGs. At 1650 hours, the Battalion was again attacked by a numerically superior NVA force. The assault was stopped through the accurate employment instructions provided by Major Duffy to US and Vietnamese tactical air strikes, as well as Cobra gunships. Enemy forces withdrew at dusk. I was relieved at 1900 hours.

On the morning of 13 April, I relieved the night shift operations officer, and according to the operations log, Major Duffy spent the remainder of the previous night and early morning of the 13th directing airstrikes against enemy staging areas and against enemy activity on Charlie One. At 1300 hours, enemy artillery fire increased against the fire base, and Major Duffy was wounded a second time in the left shoulder by shrapnel. His analysis of the LZ's critical situation was confirmed at 1645 hours when two VNAF A1-E aircraft were shot down by .51cal. AAA fire over Charlie One. At approximately 1445 hrs. Major Duffy declared the LZ untenable for use and that helicopter survivability was zero. He stated that the LZ was no longer operational and was closed. By closing the LZ, Major Duffy saved countless lives and helicopters. For the remainder of the evening, Major Duffy used artillery, tactical air force strikes, and helicopter gunships to repel enemy probes.

The situation on 14 April continued to deteriorate. An airborne company, of the 11th Airborne Battalion, was directed to find and secure an alternate evacuation LZ East of the fire base. The unit made contact with a strong NVA force, and after a sharp fight, the company was forced to withdraw to the fire base. Enemy 105mm artillery fire increased against the firebase, and while directing airstrikes under the control of a FAC call sign COVEY 537, Major Duffy was wounded a third time by shrapnel in the left arm. At 1500 hours, Major Duffy sent a message to the Brigade Senior Advisor, Major Kama, informing him that a major attack was forming, and requested demolitions be airdropped in support of the battalion's efforts to cut LZs for ammunition resupply, and evacuation of wounded.

The southwest perimeter was overrun at 1645 hours and Major Kama requested that a "Tactical Emergency (TAC-E) be declared in the II Corps area. By doing this, every aircraft, to include B-52s, would be sent to the battle area. From 1645 hours until 1830 hours, the NVA made three major assaults, and each time the 11th Battalion successfully counter-attacked. In each case, Major Duffy was the critical factor by directing Cobra gunships with devastating efficiency. The attacking gunship pilots described the NVA attacks as "human wave" assaults formations. Major Duffy reported that the battalion was out of ammunition and the Vietnamese commander was forced to order the battalion to withdraw. The unit began its withdrawal at 1840 hours. Major Duffy covered the unit's withdrawal to the northeast, using Cobra gunships (PANTHER 13/COUGAR 38) with lethal effect. During this action, the new battalion commander was seriously wounded, and Major Duffy took over command of the command group, as well as collecting survivors from the companies forced off the fire base.

Major Duffy, disregarding his painful wounds, consolidated the surviving personnel, and moved out through the darkness into the dense jungle. The survivors covered several kilometers through the night and into the next morning. During this time, Major Duffy coor-dinated AC-130 SPECTRE gunship support and through the FAC directed B-52 bomber strikes against the pursuing NVA units. At 0600 hours, Major Duffy halted the group and consolidated defen-sive positions 300 meters from the Krong River. The group was attacked by pursuing NVA units at 0700 hours. The attack caused the group to disperse and Major Duffy led the command group out of the killing zone. He coordinated with COVEY 555 for air support and helicopter extraction, and led the command group away from several ambush sites, which he detected. The extraction LZ was under direct fire and observation. The NVA continued to chase the evading survivors onto the LZ. Major Duffy guided the rescue helicopters into the LZ and was exposed to intense direct fire. As the helicopters left the LZ, the lead helicopter pilot reported that Major Duffy had been the last individual to leave the area. The exfiltration was completed at 1000 hours.

Major John J. Duffy's courage, leadership, self-sacrifice, and professionalism during the battle for Fire Support Base Charlie was unparalleled. His actions helped de-rail the NVA's time table for the Easter Offensive in the Central Highlands. He was seriously wounded and yet refused to be evacuated from his battalion. He carried out his duties while constantly subjected to direct and indirect fire. When forced off the firebase, he saved the lives of over fifty paratroopers. There is no doubt in my mind that Major Duffy's actions deserve consideration for, and the award of, the Medal of Honor.

I was present in the 2nd Airborne Brigade TOC during the battle for Fire Base Charlie and the information provided is true and correct to the best of my knowledge.
Terry A. Griswold
Major, USA RET,
1 September, 2012

Eyewitness Statement

Re: Combat Actions of the 11th Airborne Battalion in the Central Highlands at the Fire Support Base Charlie and vicinity March 30 through April 16, 1972.
Major Hai P. Doan: position at the time: Operations Officer 11th Airborne Battalion. Army of the Republic of Vietnam.
Current Residence: Milpitas, CA 95035 Citizen: USA

I was the Operations Officer of the 11th Airborne Battalion of the Army of the Republic of Vietnam. Major Duffy was the Senior Advisor to the 11th Airborne Battalion. He had campaigned with us previously and was nearing the completion of his tour. He was a very experienced advisor.

The 470 officers and men of the 11th Airborne Battalion and one American Advisor (Major Duffy) were alerted on March 30, 1972 for combat operations in the Central Highlands of Vietnam. We moved initially by aircraft to Kontum, and were then trucked north. On April 2, 1972, we combat assaulted onto Fire Support Base Charlie. Over the next seven days and nights, the enemy contacts were with the probing enemy forces during the evenings and our positions was subject to ever increasing enemy bombardments from heavy artillery, to include NVA 105mm and 130mm fire.

On the 12th of April, several command bunkers were hit by enemy artillery fire, the Battalion Commander, LTC Bao was mortally wounded, Major Me V. Le assumed command of the Battalion.

During the battle, I coordinated all supporting fire with Major Duffy. We directed artillery, Vietnamese

Air, both USAir Force and US Army strike aircraft and even B-52 bomb drops. The coordination was very effective, we got good coverage, and we annihilated many NVA attack formations. Both Major Duffy and myself were required to be continuously exposed to enemy fire while coordinating friendly air and artillery strikes.

Our situation became untenable as the NVA positioned AAA weapons to cover our Landing Zone. It quickly became obvious that we could not be resupplied with these .51caliber machine guns targeting our landing zone. Our ammunitions supply became critical and we were forced to abandon Fire Support Base Charlie.

During the evacuation, it was decided that Major Me V. Le and Major Duffy would stay behind with a small rear guard in an effort to fool the NVA into thinking that we were still manning our positions thus gaining enough time for the successful withdrawal of the battalion. The combat on FSB Charlie was intense; smoke, explosions, and screaming were the norm. Major Duffy directed the final sortie of gunships in on the enemy to cover the withdrawal. Both Majors Le and Duffy were wounded. Major Me V. Le and Major Duffy were the last two to leave the perimeter. During the break out Major Duffy was wounded in his hands and chest by enemy grenades as they pressed their attack over the walls of the compound. He continually exposed himself to enemy fire in order to direct the friendly air assets and I believe that his actions saved the survivors of our battalion during the withdrawal. Due to Major Le's serious wound, Major Duffy covered his evacuation and was the last soldier to leave FSB Charlie.

When the squad from the delaying action finally linked up with us, we found out that Major Le was seriously wounded in the chest. Major Duffy assumed command of the battalion. He immediately ordered the link-up of Company 113 who were occupying high ground of the east of our positions. Unfortunately, during the night, friendly artillery mistakenly bombarded the paratroopers, Major Duffy ordered a "check fire!" He returned command of the Battalion to Major Le as soon as he was able to continue.

The next morning, the Company Commanders reported the status of their units and we reorganized while awaiting Company 113's link-up. It was determined that Company 113 was unable to move to our position due to the large enemy units between us. Major Me V. Le gave the order for the Companies to move out being concerned that we had been in one location too long.

As we moved from our night defensive positions, the NVA initiated an ambush. The initial fire was 60mm mortar rounds and automatic weapons fire. The command scattered. Major Le and Major Duffy held the Command Group and nearby paratroopers together. Major Duffy led the break-out of the ambush, by moving rapidly through the killing zones and into the surrounding jungle. During the break-out of the ambush, we lost all radios. The only serviceable radio we had was Major Duffy's survival radio. He used it very effectively by directing air strikes on the pursuing NVA and contacted the rescue helicopters in an effort to evacuate the remaining members of the 11th Airborne Battalion. We were able to break contact with the enemy due to Major Duffy's expertise in directing gunships and moved quickly to the designated pick-up point that had been selected for us.

Major Duffy located the LZ (Landing Zone) and organized the perimeter defense. He then called for an emergency extraction on his survival radio. The first lift out took point blank machine gun fire from the south. Major Duffy worked the strike aircraft, both fixed wing and helicopter on the enemy positions. Lift two and three got in with moderate fire directed at them. Lift four, the last life was to pick up the 5 remaining survivors of the 11th Airborne Battalion: Major Duffy, Major Me, myself and 2 soldiers.

The NVA fire was extremely heavy and very accurate. After boarding the ship, I was shot in the right foot. I fell and my body seemed to be hanging in the air as I fell towards the ground. Major Duffy (who was standing on the skid of the helicopter directing air strikes), grabbed my cartridge belt as I fell past him and pulled me into the helicopter. The rescue ship temporarily lost control after being hit by anti-aircraft fire as we were pulling out. The left door gunner was hit in the chest. Major Duffy dragged him in and checked his wounds. He tried to save the door gunner by giving him mouth to mouth resuscitation, but the door gunner died in Major Duffy's arms a couple of minutes later.

Both the door gunner and I were dropped at the Medical evacuation point. I never forgot that time!!! Major Duffy was a hero commander. I often wonder what would have happened if Major Duffy had left on the first lift? The answer is very clear: we all would have died or been captured by the NVA.

Major Duffy saved my life and the 36 paratroopers that survived with him. Major Duffy risks his own life to save the 11th Airborne Battalion on the Fire Base Charlie, led the break-out of the ambush and refused to leave before all the soldiers were safely aboard the last lift.

Major Duffy saved my life and the rest of the men's lives on that landing zone. The NVA were more numerous, closing in fast and determined to kill or capture us. I estimate we were within twenty to thirty minutes of annihilation.

Major Duffy risked his own life to save us, he refused to be evacuated before all the paratroopers were safely aboard the lift ships. He led by example. Major Duffy performed in the highest traditions of bravery and he was very lucky. Major Duffy is deserving of this nation's highest award for valor: The Congressional Medal of Honor.

Signed

Respectfully submitted,

Hai P. Doan

Notarized, dated

John J. Duffy

S-T-A-T-E-M-E-N-T

This statement is to support the award nomination for John J. Duffy.

In mid-April 1972, a substantial North Vietnamese Army (NVA) force his Firebase Charlie on Rocket Ridge in the Central Highlands of South Vietnam. I was flying as pilot-in-command of an AH-1G Cobra attack helicopter that day. I was flying as the second aircraft in a fire team providing support in Kontum Province.

We received a radio call, in flight, telling us that a large enemy force, believed to be two regiments NVA were attacking Charlie with thousands of soldiers and pounding the position with barrages of 130 millimeter artillery shells. The South Vietnamese Army had a unit stationed at Charlie, the 11th Airborne Battalion. We were given a frequency and told to contact the single American advisor with the battalion, call sign "Dusty Cynanide." I later found out his name was Major John Duffy.

I was flying as wingman that day to Chief Warrant Officer Dan Jones.

We arrived at Firebase Charlie to find a very poor situation. The firebase was surrounded with the enemy advancing in strength from three sides. The South Vietnamese were fighting hard, but the enemy assault was relentless.

We fired rockets, mini-gun, and our grenade launcher on concentrations of enemy in close proximity to friendly positions. All friendly positions were being hard pressed and some being overrun. We also fired on enemy weapons positions that ringed the base. The ground fighting was the worst I have seen, and we received intense enemy fire directed against our Cobras. Major Duffy relayed that the battalion had heavy casualties and the battalion commander had been killed. He was requesting all the air support he could get. We expended our ordnance on targets that Major Duffy direct us onto, and then went to Kontum airfield to rearm and refuel.

By the time our fire team returned to Charlie, the situation had deteriorated dramatically. When we arrived, it was dusk. Major Duffy had directed other attack helicopters in our absence and employed A-1 Skyraiders and jet fighters around the firebase as well. Nonetheless, the enemy continued their attack and the situation for Major Duffy and his airborne battalion was deteriorating. The South Vietnamese defenders were being killed and their positions being overrun.

Major Duffy told us he was wounded, but would continue to work us. His focus on the radio was entirely on doing what he could for his South Vietnamese comrades. At times, while he had his microphone keyed, directing us, I could hear him giving orders to his counterparts who were fighting for their lives. I could also hear him dealing with casualties that were occurring all around him. I never heard him express any concern for himself. He would not ask for his own extraction. He seemed committed to fighting to the death with his battalion.

As the situation deteriorated further, he began asking for us to place our fire within 3 meters of his position. I have never seen greater bravery displayed in combat. His actions were affecting the best possible defense under overwhelming conditions. The fight marked one of the opening moves of the NVA's Easter Offensive. This 1972 Communist campaign turned out to be a much larger series of battles than the more well known 1968 Tet Offensive.

As darkness settled on the hilltop, the enemy overran the last remaining South Vietnamese positions of Firebase Charlie. Major Duffy called and reported he was rallying survivors and heading off the firebase. He asked us to expend our remaining ordnance right on top of the positions he was leaving. I was surprised how calm he sounded, and by his actions could tell how much in charge he remained, and how his heroic actions were the only hope for the survival of anyone left alive on the ground. Another team of Cobras from our unit, the 361st Aviation Company, joined us in the final moments of the battle, also firing on top of the base and covering the withdrawal of Major Duffy and the survivors of the battle.

While flying the next morning, I was surprised to hear radio calls for the extraction of a small element of the 11th ARVN Airborne Battalion from the valley floor east of Firebase Charlie. The badly mauled group was led by their wounded advisor, Major Duffy. The extractions were made by elements of the 17th Air Cavalry. I was amazed that anyone could have survived the concentration of North Vietnamese forces I had seen attacking Firebase Charlie. I have no doubt that without the actions of Major John Duffy as the American advisor for that unit, all would have been killed or captured.

William S. Reeder, Jr.
Colonel, U.S. Army, retired

In April 1972:
Captain, U.S. Army
Platoon Commander
361st Aviation Company, "Pink Panthers"
Camp Holloway, near Pleiku, Republic of Vietnam

John J. Duffy

S-T-A-T-E-M-E-N-T

On 14 April 1972 I was witness to acts of extraordinary heroism by Major John J. Duffy in the performance of his duties as advisor to the 11th Airborne Battalion at Firebase Charlie, Kontum Province, Vietnam. What follows is my best recollection of those events.

In the early evening of 14 April, I led a flight of two AH-1G (Cobra) gunships towards Firebase Charlie where Major Duffy was under siege by what must have been several reinforced battalions of North Vietnamese regulars (NVA). Flying my wing was another Cobra piloted by Captain Bill Reeder and his co-pilot/gunner. The battle had lasted throughout the day with many casualties suffered by the beleaguered troopers atop Charlie, including Duffy's counterpart, the Vietnamese commander.

My unit, the 361st AWC, had flown several sorties that day in support of those at Firebase Charlie as had Cobra fire teams from the 57th AHC. The area around Charlie was ringed with enemy artillery and anti-aircraft weaponry which directed a continuous barrage of fire towards both Firebase Charlie and at those of us attempting to provide relief. And in spite of apparently suffering many casualties and the loss of multiple gun positions, the enemy forces continued their assault on FSB Charlie through the afternoon and into the evening of the 14th.

Throughout the day Major Duffy provided leadership to the men of the 11th Battalion as they battled a very determined North Vietnamese force; all the while directing and coordinating the efforts of helicopter gunships and other aviation assets called in to provide air support. The enemy assault continued unabated into the evening and the situation had worsened as we approached the firebase for the last time that day.

The 11th Battalion had suffered heavy casualties and Duffy himself had been wounded. The perimeter around the firebase was breached at several points and the situation was now desperate.

As our flight of gunships approached the firebase the last light of day faded into the western horizon. I checked in on FM radio with Major Duffy. A fire team of expended 57th AHC Cobras had just departed and due to deteriorating weather, we were to be the last air cover for Duffy that day.

The situation for Duffy and his men had reached a turning point and he had made the decision to evacuate FSB Charlie. Though still in total control, he must have been exhausted in addition to being wounded. Throughout the day he had endured one of the most intense sieges of the war by motivated and well equipped NVA regulars who were determined to occupy FSB Charlie and destroy its occupants. His leadership skills and tactical acumen were on display throughout the battle. It was apparent to all of those flying in support of Major Duffy that we were witnessing heroic acts by one of the Army's finest.

As lead aircraft, I was in direct contact with Duffy who asked that we cover his withdrawal from the firebase by firing at an area he described as being on an azimuth and distance from a nearby fire. However, there were several fires and there was no way to pinpoint the exact position of Duffy and his remaining men. Upon receiving this information, he directed me to fire a pair of rockets into the hilltop so that he could adjust from the impact point.

By now, it was pitch black and our fire team was joined by a second team of 361st Cobras. We now had a flight of four, but the weather continued to deteriorate which precluded any more delay.

I picked an inbound heading and pointed the Cobra towards my best guess of the enemy position in relation to the largest fire knowing—as Duffy surely did—that this would literally be a shot in the dark. The risks from our rockets and minigun fire for Duffy and his men were high.

As the rockets reached their impact point, Major Duffy radioed "that's perfect, keep shooting there." He then continued to adjust the firepower from our team of gunships while leading his men away from the firebase to relative safety.

I am convinced that the heroic actions of Major Duffy that night caused many lives being saved as he led the few remaining survivors of the battle away from FSB Charlie and into the surrounding jungle. The group of haggard survivors apparently evaded the enemy through the remainder of the night and into the next day when they were able to be extracted by helicopter crews from another unit.

Daniel E. Jones
CW4, U.S. Army, retired

John J. Duffy

Statement
3 September 2012

To Whom It May Concern:

In the spring of 1972, I was a First Lieutenant Section Leader assigned to the 36125 Aerial Weapons Company (Airmobile) at Camp Holloway in Pleiku, Republic of Vietnam. Our radio call sign was Panther.

On 15 April 1972, I flew two missions supporting the defense of Firebase Charlie northwest of Kontum. On both of these missions, I was co-pilot/gunner in an aircraft commanded by CPT Dennis Trigg. The wing aircraft was flown by CPT Owen B. McFarland with WO1 Sam Scott as co-pilot/gunner. On both missions, our fires were directed by call sign Dusty Cyanide whom I later learned to be MAJ John Duffy.

At 1400 on 15 April, we launched from standby at Tan Canh to support Firebase Charlie and expended on a mortar position. One aircraft could shoot no rockets. We returned to Pleiku for repairs, rearm and refuel.

We were launched again at dusk on a Tactical Emergency (TAC-E) report that Firebase Charlie was being over-run. We were the second team of Panthers guns launched in response to that report.

We followed the action at Charlie on the radio as we flew northward.

While enroute, we learned that one of our fire teams (CPT Robert Gamber, Panther 26, mission lead, and 1LT Ron Lewis with copilot 1LT David Messa as wing) had been shot up at Charlie and that Charlie was under heavy ground assault. Ron tried to duke it out with a .51 and lost, taking some shrapnel in the leg. He landed safely at Vo Dinh.

As darkness fell, the Panther 26 team was replaced by a fire team from the Cougars of the 57th

Assault Helicopter company, led by Cougar 6 (CPT McDonald). We heard the American on the ground call sign Dusty Cyanide, directing their fire against massed attacks at multiple points on the perimeter and very close to his own position.

When they expended, the Cougars were replaced by the team of Panther 36 (Bill Reeder) and Panther 13 (Dan Jones). We heard Dusty Cyanide telling Bill "You broke the attack!" We also heard Bill ask where the friendlies were to which he got no answer other than "Shoot 25 meters east of the big fire."

Bill's team expended, he handed off to us, telling us that friendlies and enemy were all mixed up with each other. We put a pair of rockets 50 meters east of the largest fire in the middle of multiple large and small fires and were told "That's it Panther. Put it right there!" then, a shout through an open mike, "Keep your head down!" Then "OK Panther, you broke the attack." Then, out of breath, "We're clearing out. Put it all right there!" We put the rest of our load between the big fire and the assumed position of the friendlies. The next thing we heard from the out-of-breath voice was "You broke the attack. We're clear, heading down the mountain," and then nothing.

When the survivors had been recovered, Dusty Cyanide sent his gratitude via news man Peter Arnett. The message was "Those first guns were good. They broke the attack. But that last team was shit hot. They broke things up and covered our escape." Peter Arnett came by our Company Club to deliver the message in person.

Forrest B. Snyder, Jr.
MAJ, USAR Retired
In 1972: 1LT, FA, Section Leader,
361st Aerial Weapons Company

Statement

My name is James M Gibbs, LTC, USA (Ret). In April 1972, I commanded H Trp (Air) 17th Cav stationed at Camp Holloway, Pleiku, South Vietnam. This was the period of the NVA and Viet Cong forces build up to take Kontum and other strategic locations to later overrun and take control of South Vietnam.

On Apr 15, 1972 our mission was to go to Kontum for a mission in that area. While enroute we learned that Fire Support Base (FSB) Charlie had been overrun the night before. We understood that a US advisor, later determined to be Maj John Duffy, and many of the ARVN soldiers at that FSB had escaped with limited arms and ammunition and were evading the enemy forces pursuing them. Radio contact was made with an USAF forward air controller (FAC) who was in contact with Maj Duffy. The FAC related that an extraction was urgently needed. (I do not recall how or if I got released from the original mission.) The FAC was providing air support and communications for Maj Duffy and his soldiers. Cobra gunships from my unit were sent to provide additional close fire support and assess the situation. Enroute it was determined that Maj Duffy had 37 ARVN (4 wounded) with him to be extracted. There were 4 UH-1 troop carrying helicopters (slicks) available in the immediate area including my C&C slick.
The USAF FAC turned control over to one of my gunships to direct us in and provide covering fire. Radio contact was established between Maj Duffy

on the ground, the gunship lead, and the slicks. Maj Duffy had led the ARVN soldiers numerous miles and hours from FSB Charlie while evading the enemy, coming under fire frequently. He briefed us on where the enemy was and that every time they approached a possible clearing to be used as a LZ they would come under fire. He identified an LZ and used smoke to mark the site. He then directed each slick into the site and ensured they and the gunships knew where the enemy fire would be expected from.

Maj Duffy's composure, knowledge of the situation and those ARVN soldiers with him, coupled with his leadership under enemy fire was undoubtedly responsible for the extraction of all those with him. His decision to remain for the last aircraft to be personally extracted, knowing the inherent risk to his own life, ensured those he was responsible for had the best chance to survive. His selflessness continued even when he boarded that last aircraft by ensuring those wounded while getting aboard under fire were administered medical care.

James M. Gibbs, LTC USA (RET)

STATEMENT

My name is Dennis Watson. At the time of this event, April 15, 1972, I was a 21-year old WO1 flying co-pilot for the Commander of 7/17 Air Cav Squadron, Maj. Mike Gibbs. Our UH 1 was tasked to serve as the Command and Control aircraft from which the operation would be directed.

A recording, made by myself, is provided. The fact that I recorded this flight resulted from a conversation I had a few days prior with our Chaplain to seek his advice about managing stressful personal emotions. He asked if I had a wife..yes...if I confided in her...no. He sternly advised me to do so. Hence, I would record a mission, knowing how unlikely it was that anything but the normal boring flight would take place. Using a cassette recorder I plugged the earphone into the microphone jack so that it operated as a microphone. I then placed the piece inside the ear cup of my helmet, not inserted into my ear. It then recorded every comment made on the radio as well as muffled ambient noises.

As our group of helicopters flew from Camp Holloway to Kontum we began to hear "chatter" on the universal "guard" frequency. Ground forces from Firebase Charlie were communicating with a Forward Air Controller. In time we learned that the Firebase Charlie had been under assault for three days before being overrun on April 15, An American Major (John Duffy—call sign "Dusty Cyanide") whose name I would not learn for more than 30 years, led the evasion of approximately 35 soldiers. Maj. Gibbs dispatched two of our Cobras to the area to provide fire support while the other aircraft refueled, at which time Maj. Gibbs requested and was given a change of mission.

Maj. Duffy's voice was completely inconsistent with the reality of the circumstances. He was completely calm and in complete control as he directed the fire from our Cobras, directed our flight to his location, interacted with the FAC, and directed his troops.

The first Huey landed and took off with his load but Maj. Duffy did not board it. His intentions became immediately apparent. I have no doubt he expected the LZ to become very "hot." Being the only American, he feared American pilots would be less likely to risk a hot LZ to extract Vietnamese rather than an American. He knew that as the Hueys continued to land the enemy would know the paths in and out and would be able to assemble themselves accordingly. By remaining on the ground, Maj. Duffy, in effect, offered his life in exchange for those of his men. As the odds of losing a Huey increased, the odds of his own survival decreased. The Hueys continued to land, taking sporadic fire. As our aircraft, 4th and final, approached the LZ, Maj Duffy continued to direct us to his position in his calm, clear voice. On short final we began taking heavy ground fire and aborted the landing. It would be years later that I would learn that the NVA knew John Duffy's name as well as that of the Command Group who were with him. The NVA were determined they would not escape.

As we made our second approach into the landing zone I observed a B-40 grenade pass in front of the helicopter. Maj Duffy directed us to his tree-line location. They were taking fire as they ran for the helicopter but Maj Duffy stayed with his men as they covered the distance. As they neared the aircraft we began taking hits into the cockpit, one of which struck and killed one of our Door Gunners, Dallas Nihsen. I believe every man who boarded our helicopter was wounded but am certain one Vietnamese was. As we departed the LZ Maj Duffy moved about the aircraft administering first aid, first to Dallas, then to others.

From the first moment I heard his voice until the last, Maj. Duffy was a skilled, fearless leader who was selfless to the end. But, beyond his obvious skills and leadership, I consider none great than his ultimate act, that of willingly offering his life for the lives of his men.

John J. Duffy

STATEMENT

Nam Nhat Phan
Captain, Army of the Republic of Vietnam
Academy Military, Dalat (1963)
1963-1971 Platoon Leader, Company Commander, Operations Officer, Airborne Division
1971-1972 Press Officer, Ranger Headquarters
1973-1975 Operations Officer, Joint Military 2 and 4 Party Committee
1975-1989 Prisoner, Communist Concentration Camps (I was isolated 1979-1988 in underground confinement.)

As the Press Officer for the Ranger Headquarter, I contacted Doctor (Captain) To Pham Lie who had just come back from "Charlie" Base. Kontum Province in the Highlands of Central Vietnam. Doctor To was at the Airborne Division Medical Center treating the many wounded who had just returned with him from the battle.

I tape-recorded all the details of the battle for "Charlie" Base. I additionally interviewed the survivors, and assembled these battlefield heroics of the participants from the eyewitnesses.

They particularly talked about Major Duffy and his bravery, and about his rescue of the 11th Battalion men.

The Story of "Charlie" Base was transmitted throughout all of South Vietnam by Voice of Vietnam Radio, Army Radio in Saigon, and through all of South Vietnam by local radio stations.

My recordings and interviews were assembled and re-edited into a book. "The Red Flames of Summer" received wide acclaim and was awarded the 1972

National Literature Award. Doctor To Pham Lieu is now deceased, but he was an eyewitness to the "Charlie" Base battle. In "The Red Flames of Summer" I recorded these events as told to me by eyewitnesses. The "Charlie" segment of the book has been translated into English, thus the board can read it; this is bringing back a witness from the past.

I should also state that the Vietnamese people had very few American heroes. Major Duffy is one of them because of his unselfish and extremely brave actions in this "Charlie" battle.

English translation by Vann Saroyan Phan
signed
notarized

Translation Excerpts

Duffy, running amid smoke and dust with a radio on his back, was issuing short, clear and precise orders. And from the sky, silvery jet fighters, with their fierce firepower were diving down on the enemy hidden in the dark, smoky words. As the jets cleared away, Cobra gunships came in. The noise of bombs, anti-aircraft guns, rockets, heavy guns and mortars shook the broken red-clay hill.

Like in a Hollywood combat scene, wherever Duffy went, enemy fire followed him. And he immediately moved to another position. "Shit!" Major Me Le shouted into Hai's ears. "Get someone to tell Duffy to lie down because his antenna is being targeted." It was a moment too late. Duffy's tall body was lifted off the ground and thrown into a trench.

Like a miracle, from the mess of soil, rock, dust and smoke, the study man stood up and ran to another position, the receiver of his radio still in his hand. "Over! Over!" There was still no change in his voice.

* * * * *

Major Me Le, the executive officer of the battalion, did not bother to think of the number of weapons taken from the enemy by companies 1 and 3. The command bunker of Colonel Bao had taken a direct hit by three big shells. No one in there could survive the explosion. After Colonel Bao died, Major Me Le replaced him as battalion commander. The duty was heavy for him since the situation seemed critical Me Le, Hai, and Dr. Lieu, the battalion surgeon, looked at one another. Night was falling and the warriors were spent. Duffy lay unconscious with a concussion, his receiver hanging loose and the radio buzzing into the darkness.

It was not a calm and silent night for them. A unit of communist sappers attacked the northernmost outpost of Company 3, aiming to clear the way for another attack on Fire Support Base Charlie.

Driven by a miraculous strength, Duffy stood up with his radio in hand, using his personal frequency. Because of the darkness, aircraft that were effective in daylight were rendered ineffective. Duffy had to rely on another weapon: the armed Spectre C130. From a hole in the night sky, the "fire dragon" directed by Duffy, let off a volley of endless fire and smoke on the dark jungle below. The fire licked a circle around the base. The fire shed light on the attacking Northerners. The day was approaching but nobody could notice it since smoke from the night fires had blurred the sunshine. Duffy spent another sleepless night, his radio by his side all the time.

The Last Day of the Battle for "Charlie"

The NVA had surrounded "Charlie" with anti-aircraft guns. The fighters were out of water, food, and ammunition. No re-supply was possible, as the guns surrounded "Charlie." There were many wounded among the paratroopers. Dr. Lieu was busy administering to them as best he could.

The situation was desperate, Major Me Le, Captain Doan and Duffy held a counsel. It was determined that the anti-aircraft guns and the artillery guns had to be taken out, because without resupply they would not be able to fight.

Major Me Le asked Duffy," Can you knock out the guns?"

Duffy said, "As long as I can get strike aircraft, I'll get them, but I need covering fire while I target the strikes.

Me Le told Hai, "See that Duffy's covered and have someone good spot the guns for him!"

Hai Doan responded, "It will be done."

They were thirsty, hungry and full of the grime and the blood of the battle. The mood among the commanders was grim and determined. They would not give up "Charlie."

Duffy, with Hai helping with the targets, went to the edge of the perimeter with his radio and began directing the airstrikes. He went after the guns, one after another. The NVA had spotted him and were targeting his radio antenna. He was wounded again early in the morning, but he kept on, ignoring his wounds. Duffy always kept moving, seeking the enemy and calling the bombs from the aircraft down on them.

He knocked out five anti-aircraft guns and three artillery pieces that were shelling "Charlie." The battle built up all day long. It was clear that the NVA were determined to take "Charlie."

The attack came early in the evening. It was a mass wave assault by a battalion size force. Hundreds of enemy rounds tore into "Charlie" base. Duffy continued to direct the silver jets and the sleek Cobra gunships. The fighters fought until they had no more bullets. Then they died fighting with grenades, knives and empty rifles, which were now used as clubs.

The aircraft punished and held off the attacking enemy. Major Me Le and Duffy were in the forefront, commanding the battle. Me ordered counter-attacks three times. Duffy worked the gunfire ever closer. The scene was one of noise and smoke and fear.

The enemy pushed two more battalions into the battle and "Charlie" began to crumble. Only the planes held the enemy back.

The Retreat of the Battalion from "Charlie"

At last, Major Me Le, Hai, and Duffy came to a decision: They would abandon Charlie by late afternoon on April 14. Duffy volunteered to stay behind and cover the withdrawal. Major Me Le agreed and ordered Hai to lead the withdrawal as night began to descend.

Duffy covered the withdrawal by working the Cobras in the trench lines that the NVA were using the advance. He gunned them down as they tried to overwhelm his position. When the troops had withdrawn, only Duffy remained with Major Me Le covering him. Then they broke contact and ran for their lives. Duffy asked for some B-52 sorties on the east and west of the firebase. When the battalion was 400 meters away from the base, the bombs started to fall. The whole unit lay struggling on the slope because of the high pressure created by the explosions, which felt like an earthquake. The terrible tremor was felt from everybody's feet and chest. Me Le bent his body down in pain from his wound. Hai spat out clots of dried blood. Dr. Lieu lay motionless by the foot of a tree.

As Duffy was the only officer still in good shape, he temporarily replaced Me Le as commander for the night retreat. Duffy was the last resort of the whole battalion and actually he was the last soldier on the way out. Artillery fire mistakenly bombarded the friendly troops as they were withdrawing, Duffy "checked fire," but not before more fighters were killed.

On the morning of April 15, Me Le chose a clearing by the Poko River for the battalion to fetch water and to evacuate the wounded. An empty space among the reeds was their last hope after seven days and nights under heavy bombardment and human wave attacks by two communist regiments at Firebase Charlie. Me Le requested lift evacuation, however, the Brigade said there would be no evacuation helicopters and ordered the battalion to fight its way back to Tan Canh. But how could the airborne unit continue to fight with the remaining 167 men, including the wounded who were hungry and mostly out of ammunition?

Me Le asked Duffy to come to him as the American advisor was following Hai and Dr. Lieu. After being wounded five times in four days of fighting and with little sleep, Duffy was still hard as steel.

"You're number one," Dr. Lieu said to Duffy as the man walked past Hai to be with Me Le.

"Hello Doc!" Duffy smiled at the battalion surgeon.

"Hey, Duffy!" The brigade had no chopper for us. Our only hope is you." Me Le was unable to continue with what he really wanted to say.

The American advisor grasped the idea quickly. "OK! Ten minutes, Sir!" said Duffy, who gave a thumbs-up.

But no more than "ten minutes" for the 11th Battalion. From the elevations in the east, NVA gunners unleashed mortar and mountain artillery down on the airborne unit while enemy troops were attacking from the southeast. Without trenches, out of ammunition, tired, hungry and thirsty for four days, men from the 11th Battalion had endured the utmost suffering. They rolled over, moved back and forth and were dying amid the reeds and under the merciless shelling and shooting.

"Surrender, you'll survive! Fight back, you'll die!" the Northerners shouted as they rushed into the battle like a dike broken away by flood. The whole battalion suffered the fate of an exhausted bear bitten by extremely poisonous bees. The unit fell apart into small fragments, each fought by itself. The voice of both sides yelling and shouting as the onslaught shook the jungle which was already filled with dark smoke.

Me Le declared, "No Surrender. We Fight!"

Duffy said, "I'll lead. You cover me." and the breakout began. Duffy gathered all the fighters who hadn't fled, cocked his CAR-15 and sprinted northeast, away from the killing guns, with 36 following.

It was like a miracle when Duffy succeeded in making contact with two Cobra gunships and an 02 observer plane. Thanks to the empty terrain of the wood and following the direction of Duffy, the Cobras could see clearly enough to fire and drive the enemy out of the clearing.

The remaining 36 men were divided into groups for evacuation.

A helicopter hastily landed on the edge of the wood. The pilot just wanted to evacuate Duffy first. But the man made a quick decision. Duffy told Hai, Me and Dr. Lieu. "I won't abandon you, friends in the fullest meaning I've ever met. If I leave on the first lift, the helicopter might not want to return to pick you up."

Me Le gave orders: "Lieu, you go first. You have a wound on your leg and you won't be able to run. Take the seriously wounded with you on the first lift.

"I won't go. I'll stay with you," Lieu protested.

"You must leave! That's an order!"

Hai pushed Lieu onboard the chopper. Lieu turned his head back to his friends. His eyes expressed sorrow and guilt. He did not know if they would live. The enemy was close and firing at them.

The communist troops ran toward those who remained on the ground. The whole group fired back, running. Cobras gave effective close support for the next two lifts. So the last group included Me Le, Duffy, Hai and Lt. Long. The communists called Me Le, Hai, and Duffy by their names. They were trying to capture alive the battalion commander and his staff, along with the American advisor.

The last lift helicopter was coming in for the pick-up. The enemy was once again shooting at them from close range with automatic weapons. Duffy covered the command group with his weapon, saying, "Go! Go! Go!" All the time Duffy talked to the Cobras and they made killing runs on the NVA. The command group scrambled aboard the aircraft. Bullets were tearing through the metal Duffy jumped onto the strut and gave the pilot the lift-off signal.

Captain Hai was hit as the chopper lifted off and was falling out. Duffy grabbed him and with Me Le's help, pulled him back aboard. The door-gunner had been hit in the chest. The pilot struggled to evade enemy fire as the chopper was riddled with bullets. Duffy tried to patch the hole in the door-gunner's chest, but he died in Duffy's arms.

* * * * *

End of Excerpt.

SECTION III

BIOGRAPHIES

General Fred C. Weyand
LTC Peter Kama
LTC Me Van Le
Major Terry A. Griswold
Major Hai P. Doan
Colonel William S. Reeder, Jr.
CW4 Daniel E. Jones
Major Forest B. Snyder, Jr.
LTC James M. Gibbs
Captain Nam Nhat Phan
CW4 Dennis Watson

John J. Duffy

GENERAL FREDERICK C. WEYAND

General Frederick C. Weyand, the last Commander of the Military Advisor Command, Vietnam, fought the big battles of the Vietnam War. As Corps Commander in the 1968 Tet Offensive, he was key in redeploying forces prior to the attack, thereby blunting the effectiveness of the enemy. The Easter Offensive of 1972 saw the entire North Vietnamese Army on the attack on three separate fronts. Tanks, heavy artillery, radar controlled anti-aircraft guns, and anti-aircraft missiles were all employed. The allies were successful, but suffered extensive casualties. The siege of An Loc went on for over 60 days as did the Battle of Quang Tri in the north.

The NVA lost more than half their attacking force of 150,000 plus the majority of their equipment. The South Vietnamese suffered heavy casualties in the initial assault, but once air support was employed effectively, the tide turned. In the process of fighting the battles, as deputy to General Abrams, Weyand was also drawing down the allied forces. The war was turned over to the Vietnamese per direction of Congress after this campaign was finished. Without adequate logistics, the Vietnamese were defeated in 1975 and a great exodus took place.

Prior to commanding the theater, General Weyand served in the Burma theatre in WWII and commanded a battalion in the Korean War. In Vietnam, he commanded the 25th Division and a Corps. He was without question the most experience General Officer of the Vietnam War era. He also served two years as military advisor to the U.S. peace negotiators in Paris.

He went on to head the Pacific Command and became the 28th Chief of Staff of the U.S. Army, retiring in 1976. He served in various civic positions until his death on February 10, 2010.

His decorations for valor include the Distinguished Service Cross and the Silver Star. General Weyand was a "soldier's soldier," he led from the front. He served his country for over sixty years. His final resting place is in the "Punchbowl" in his beloved Hawaii.

LTC LE VAN ME

LTC Le Van Me, a legendary leader in his country's war against the north was a native of the old imperial capital of Hue. He attended the Dalat Military Academy and was commissioned in 1961.

He served with the elite paratrooper Division for fourteen years. He fought in all the major battles of the war, serving in command positions. As Commander of the 11th Battalion, he distinguished himself in both the Kontum Battle and the Battle for Quang Tri in the north.

He was awarded more than twenty valor awards, including his nation's highest award—the National Order of Vietnam – Knight (fifth class), The Vietnam Army Distinguished Service Order (second class), seven Gallantry Crosses with palm, plus six Gallantry Crosses with Gold, Silver, or Bronze Stars. He was wounded three times and is one of Vietnam's most decorated soldiers. U.S. medals he was awarded include the Silver Star and the Bronze Star for Valor.

He was serving as the Operations Officer of the Airborne Division when Saigon fell in 1975 and barely managed to escape with his wife, Sen, and their three young children. After seven days on a small, derelict boat, they were rescued and taken to the United States where they settled in the San Jose area of California. His fourth child was born a couple of weeks after arriving in the United States.

He worked in Silicon Valley and simultaneously pursued an electrical engineering degree in night school. In his 28-year career as an engineer, he rose in position to Senior Manager, R&D Senior Manager and Director. He retired from Samsung of America in 2004. He holds seven patents and has made significant contributions in the storage memory field.

Le Van Me now devotes his time to his beautiful wife, Sen, and his family. His children include a journalist, an engineer, a lawyer, and a teacher. His grandchildren are all a great joy to him and Sen. He stays in shape by running marathons and half-marathons.

LTC PETER KAMA

LTC Peter Kama, a native Hawaiian, entered the Army in 1954 and was commissioned in 1956. He served in Europe, Korea, and close to four years in Vietnam.

In Vietnam he performed from village level to Company, Battalion and Brigade command. He served as aide to General Weyand, the last Commander in the Vietnam War.

His role as advisor to an Airborne brigade during the intense battles of the Easter Offensive of 1972 were noteworthy. He played a critical role in stopping the enemy in the Central Highlands and later in the northern Quang Tri region. He is credited with destroying two NVA tank regiments (119 tanks) in that battle. He is one of the most combat-experienced leaders from the Vietnam era.

LTC Kama retired from the Army in 1975 and went back to school briefly. He was called upon to be the Military Technical Advisor to the film, "Apocalypse Now" which is an American classic about the Vietnam War. He also worked in the newspaper industry for thirteen years.

Upon retirement, he returned to his native Hawaii where he served as President of a Native Medical Health Facility for eleven years, expanding both services and budget more than tenfold.

Currently he is working to expand and implement the Hawaiian Homeland Act to benefit native Hawaiians.

Pete is an avid golfer, family man, and active member of his church.

MAJOR HAI DOAN

Major Hai Doan was born on April 1, 1943, in Ha Noi (North Vietnam). In 1954, he immigrated to Saigon (South Vietnam) with his family. He graduated from the National Military Academy, Da Lat, Class of 1964.

Throughout his ten-year military career, he served in the Airborne Division, first in the 7th Battalion and in the 11th Battalion.

Hai has been engaged in many fierce battles, including the battle of Dong Xoài, Ha Lào, Charlie, Binh Gia, Khe Sanh, Kontum, Pleiku, and Quang Tri. He was wounded three times in battle.

Hai has been honored with seventeen awards and decorations, including The National Order of Vietnam Knight Class, four Gallantry Crosses with Palm, five Gallantry Crosses with Star, and three Wounded Medals, and the U.S. bronze Star with Valor.

On April 30, 1975, when Saigon fell to the Communists, Hai and his family immigrated to the United States.

In 1978, he graduated from Silicon Valley Technical Institute. Hai worked as an Electronics Engineer for companies such as Data Point, Ampex, National Semiconductor, and Silicon Graphics. He retired in 2004 after a 26-year career in electronics.

Hai is currently living in San Jose, California with his wife, children, and four grandchildren. He enjoys reading and writing. He has written for several Vietnamese magazines, newspapers, short story books, and was the Chief Editor of Vietnamese Da Hieu magazine.

Published Books:
Góc Bien Chân Troi (2000)
Nho ve...Nguoi Linh Nam Xua (2011)

TERRY GRISWOLD, MAJOR (retired)

As a young officer, Terry Griswold served in the biggest battles of the Vietnam war with courage and distinction. He led patrols behind enemy lines, directed rescues, and worked the critical airstrikes only Americans were authorized to direct.

Post Vietnam, he served more than twenty years in the Army and served with elite Special Forces, Special Operations units, and Intelligence.

Terry retired as a Major. He went on to become a Corporate Consultant for special operations, counter-narcotics and counter-terrorism.

Terry co-authored the definitive book: "Delta, America's Elite Counter-Terrorist Force," available on Amazon.

Terry is currently retired and lives in Kansas with his wife, Debbie.

COLONEL WILLIAM ("Bill") REEDER

During the battle of Firebase Charlie, Captain Bill Reeder was a flight platoon leader in the 361st Aerial Weapons Company based out of Camp Holloway, near Pleiku, Republic of Vietnam. On April 14, 1972, he was flying as wingman to Chief Warrant Officer Dan Jones, supporting "Dusty Cyanide" (Major John Joseph Duffy) fighting for his life and the survival of the 11th Airborne Battalion. Bill and Dan flew two heavily armed AH-1G Cobra attack helicopter gunships as Panther 13 flight.

Bill was commissioned from Officer Candidate School. He was a college dropout who had worked as a ranch hand, a firefighter for the Forest Service, and as an electrical lineman for Southern California Edison before enlisting in the Army. He was shot down flying OV-1 Mohawk reconnaissance airplanes deep behind enemy lines on his first tour of duty in Vietnam. He returned two years later to fly Cobra gunships.

Just three weeks after the fight at Firebase Charlie, Bill was shot down at the nearby camp at Ben Het. He was captured by the Communist North Vietnamese. He spent nearly a year as a prisoner of war, being released at the end of March 1973. Interestingly, one of the Vietnamese Air Force pilots flying an A-1 Skyraider in support at Firebase Charlie, Nguyen Xanh, was shot down the same day as Bill, and they spent time together in a POW camp and traveling north together on the Ho Chi Minh Trail—an arduous death march to Hanoi.

After release from captivity at the end of the war, Bill returned to active service as an Army officer and aviator. Subsequent assignments included various command and staff positions, and a stint at the U.S. Air Force Academy. He commanded at all levels, platoon through brigade (including command on an AH-64 Apache attack helicopter squadron). His last assignment before retirement in 1995 was as the Deputy Chief of Staff, de facto Chief of Staff, for the United States Southern Command in Panama. He retired from the Army as a full Colonel.

Upon completing his Army career, Bill returned to school and earned a Ph.D. in history with an additional field of study in anthropology. He served as a professor and Deputy Director of the U.S. Army School of Advanced Military Studies (SMS), and later as Chief of Leader Development for I Corps at Fort Lewis, Washington. He now spends parts of each year in the education of NATO Special Operations Forces at the NATO SOF School at Chievres Air Base, Belgium.

His military awards and decorations include the Valorous Unit Award, Defense Superior Service Medal, Legion of Merit, two Distinguished Flying Crosses, and three Bronze Star medals, three Purple Hearts for wounds received in action, the POW Medal, Vietnamese Cross of Gallantry with Bronze Star, and numerous Air Medals (one with "V" device). In 1977 he was named Army Aviator of the Year. He was featured in the PBS documentary, "The Helicopter Pilots of Vietnam" and has provided military commentary on CNN and the Discovery Channel.

Bill is married to the former Melanie Lineker of Westminster, Maryland, who is also a retired Army Colonel and works as the Director of Training (N-7) for the **U.S. Navy Northwest Region, headquartered at Bangor Submarine Base, Washington. They have four children.**

CW4 DAN JONES

At the time of the battle for Firebase Charlie, CW2 Dan Jones was assigned to the 3rd Platoon of the 361st Aerial Weapons Company, operationally known as the "Pink Panthers." He was a designated Cobra aircraft commander and air mission commander. Mr. Jones' other duties with the 361st included that of Aviation Safety Officer, UH-1 Instructor Pilot, and Instrument Instructor Pilot.

One the afternoon of 14 April 1972, with Captain Bill Reeder flying wing position, Dan led an AH-1G Cobra fire team that destroyed four anti-aircraft guns in head-to-head duels. After refueling and re-arming, Dan and Bill returned to the battle, providing covering fire, "under the enemies' guns." They broke the enemy assault on the rear guard led by the Advisor and were crucial in saving the remnants of the Vietnamese Army's 11th Airborne Battalion. The battalion in a night retrograde movement off of "FSB Charlie," was under direct assault from two NVA battalions. Though flying in total darkness and with inclement weather closing in, Dan's team of gunships provided deadly and accurate close air support to those fighting for their lives inside the firebase perimeter. Major Duffy directed and adjusted the Cobra's weaponry as necessary to give his men a chance to survive the enemy onslaught and escape into the nearby jungle.

Dan was born and raised in Tucson, Arizona, and as a third generation Arizonan, his roots are traceable to a line of pioneering ancestors who helped settle the area as homesteaders and political leaders during the state's early history. His great-grandfather served in the first legislature after statehood was granted in 1912.

From early in his childhood, Dan was influenced by an uncle who flew B-17s as a nineteen year-old and later spent time as a POW during WWII. Dan was determined to be a pilot as well. As a young man and as the war in Vietnam developed, he went to school, first attending Eastern Arizona College, then the University of Arizona.

Dan chose to enlist in the Army for Warrant Officer Flight School in early 1967. Following basic training at Ft. Polk, Louisiana, and primary helicopter training at Ft. Wolters, Texas, he earned his wings in March, 1968 at Ft. Rucker, Alabama, graduating with Class 67-503.

Like so many other pilots in the 361st, Dan was serving a second tour of duty in Vietnam, having spent his first tour with the 1st Cavalry Division, initially with the 229th Assault Helicopter Battalion. It was during the Division's assault of the Ashau Valley (Operation Delaware) in April of 1968 that Dan's helicopter became one of twelve shot down during the first day of the battle. Then, a few months later, while descending into an LZ, he and his crew were ambushed and the UH-1 Huey was raked with machine gun fire which wounded all on board but Dan, who flew the damaged helicopter and crew to safety. Then, while hovering over another LZ a few weeks later, his Huey experienced a tail rotor failure. The spinning helicopter landed on a steep slope and rolled onto its side.

Dan was selected as Chief Pilot for a Battalion Commander and managed to stay above the battlefield until rotation, returning to CONUS with orders for the Primary Helicopter School at Ft. Wolters, Texas as a flight instructor. Later, he was assigned to the Methods of Instruction/Flight Standards Department as a Standardization Flight Evaluator, administering check rides to student pilots as they progressed through the various phases of flight school. With an eye to the future, Dan took fixed wing flying lessons in his spare time and soon achieved ratings in single and multi-engine fixed wing airplanes.

Before returning to Vietnam for his second tour of duty, Dan received orders for AH-1G Cobra transition at Ft. Hunter, Georgia, as well as the Aviation Safety Officers course at the University of Southern California. Being equipped with these two new qualifications, Dan was uniquely suited for assignment to the 361st AWC upon returning to Vietnam for the second time.

In mid-April, at the time of the spring offensive by the NVA and the associated events taking place at Fire Base Charlie, Dan was getting very close to completion of his second tour in Vietnam. Later that month he left that country for the last time and proceeded to his next assignment with the 101st Airborne at Ft. Campbell, Kentucky. In June 1972, Dan requested and was granted his release from active duty in July 1972.

During his two tours of duty in Vietnam, Dan received several awards and decorations, including the Distinguished Flying Cross (OLC), Vietnam Cross of Gallantry (Gold Star), Air Medal (39 OLC), Air Medal (Valor), Army Commendation Medal (Valor), Purple Heart, and Bronze Star (OLC).

Back in Arizona, Dan moved to Phoenix and enrolled at Arizona State University. He joined the Arizona National Guard's 997th Aviation Company (Assault Helicopter) as a UH-1H pilot. Later, he was assigned to the gun platoon which operated UH-1M gunships.

While attending classes in Aviation Management Technology, Dan began part-time work as a research assistant and course coordinator for the Crash Research Institute at the ASU College of Engineering. There he assisted with studies and engineering research associates with the crashworthiness aspects of aviation and vehicular accidents. The institute also trained accident investigators from military, government, and civilian organizations, with emphasis on crash survivability. The research produced at CRI led directly to the development of new technology that paved the way for crashworthy fuel systems as well as other design improvements in seat and constraint systems applicable to aircraft and automobiles.

When a full-time position with the National Guard as a helicopter flight instructor opened at the Army Aviation Support Facility, Dan was hired. He began full-time status in 1979 under the Active Guard/Reserve (AGR) program which had recently been created by the Department of the Army. Located in Phoenix at the Papago Army Airfield, the full-time position came with a transition into fixed wing aircraft which allowed Dan to gain additional experience.

In the early Eighties, the Arizona National Guard began f fielding newly renovated Cobras to replace the older UH-1M helicopters. Dan was part of the cadre of instructors who helped transition the unit's part-time pilots into the newer airframe. Then, in the mid-80s, the ASSF developed a program to qualify all pilots in the use of night vision devices. As a Night Vision Goggle IP, Dan logged over 400 hours of flight instruction over the next several years in addition to his other duties.

Late in 1991, Dan and another pilot flew a UN-1H to Helena, Montana to be checked out in "Bambi Bucket" operations by the Montana National Guard. After several sorties of dipping water from the Missouri River, then releasing it over imaginary fires, Dan became the designated Bambi Bucket IP for the ASEF in Arizona.

In July of 1994, Dan flew a helicopter for the last time. The mission was in support of firefighters near Kingman, Arizona, who were attempting to suppress a wildfire.

Dan's final job assignment in the military was with Detachment 31, Operational Support Airlift Command (OSAC) flying C-12 fixed wing aircraft. He served there until his retirement from the U.S. Army on 31 January, 1996.

Over his 23 years with the Arizona National Guard, Dan's duties included: Standardization Instructor Pilot, Qualification Instructor Pilot, Instrument Flight Examiner, Unit Safety Officer, and fixed wing pilot. He never crashed or damaged another helicopter.

After retirement from the National Guard, Dan worked as a charter pilot for Cutter Aviation, Phoenix, flying turboprop and jet aircraft. After four years with Cutter, he was hired by Empire South, an Arizona Caterpillar dealer, to fly their company airplanes and he remained there for the next eight years.

Currently, Dan is a corporate pilot for DriveTime, an auto dealer headquartered in Phoenix with stores located through the United States. He has accumulated over 16,000 hours of flight time over an aviation career spanning five decades.

In his spare time, Dan is fond of mountain biking and gardening. He is married to the former Carole Sheppard whose family is rooted in Wilmington, Delaware and St. Louis, Missouri. She is an avid and capable genealogist. They have four children: three girls and a boy, as well as five grandchildren.

LTC JOHN G. ("JACK") HESLIN

In 1972, during the Battle of Kontum, as a US Army Captain, Jack served as the 52nd Combat Aviation Battalion S-3 and the 17th Combat Aviation Group Assistant S-3. During the battle, he flew various missions to include the AIR BOSS mission which had responsibility to coordinate all aviation assets coming into the battle area around Kontum City. While flying that mission, Jack used FOB 2, located just south of Kontum City, as a refueling point when flying the AIR BOSS mission — call sign "SAGE STREET."

Details of the Battle of Kontum can be found on Jack's website: www.TheBattleofKontum.com.

Jack attended high school at La Salle Academy and graduated from Providence College in Providence, Rhode Island, with a Bachelor of Arts Degree in Sociology. He was commissioned in the Regular Army on 1 June 1965 and married Jean Savoie Heslin on 5 June 1965. Jean and Jack have four children, with eight grandchildren.

In 1965 Jack attended Infantry Officer Basic Course and Airborne Training at Fort Benning, Georgia and was assigned to the 82nd Airborne Division where he served as a platoon leader in the Dominican Republic and commanded the rear detachment for 1st Battalion, 504th Infantry at Fort Bragg, North Carolina.

After attending Rotary Wing Flight School from October 1966 through June 1967, Jack was assigned to the 57th Assault Helicopter Company at Fort Bragg and deployed with the unit to Vietnam in October 1967. He served as an assault helicopter platoon commander and operations officer for the 119th Assault Helicopter Company.

Following completion of his first tour in Vietnam, he was assigned to the U.S. Army Aviation Center at Fort Rucker, Alabama, where he performed duties as a senior instruction for the Warrant Officer Career Course and commanded the 31st Enlisted Student Company.

After completing the Infantry Officer Advanced Course as an honor graduate in July 1971, Jack attended Fixed Wing Transition Training on his way to a second tour in Vietnam. In Vietnam, he performed duties as the 52nd Combat Aviation Battalion S-3, operations officer, and Assistant S-3 for the 17th Combat Aviation Group during the period December 1971 through December 1972.

Upon returning from Vietnam, Jack attended the University of Rhode Island and completed a Master's Degree in Sociology and graduated with honors in 1974. After completing the Master's Degree, Jack assumed duties as an ROTC instructor at the University of Rhode Island for a period of three years. In 1977, Jack attended the Naval War College Command and Staff Course and graduated with honors in June 1978.

After aviator refresher training at Fort Rucker, Alabama, Jack served with the 3rd Squadron, 4th Cavalry, 25th Infantry Division Hawaii, October 1978. Jack was the 3rd Squadron S-3 for one year and commander of C Troop for one year before joining Headquarters Western Command as the Aviation Officer, DCSOPS, in December 1980.

Jack was assigned to Fort Lee, Virginia in August 1981 as the Chief, Operations & Tactics Branch Chief of the Unit and special projects officer before retiring on December 31, 1985.

LTC Heslin has been awarded the Silver Star, the Distinguished Flying Cross, the Bronze Star Medal with oak leaf cluster, the Air Medal with "V" device and 24 oak leaf clusters, the Meritorious Service Medal with three oak leaf clusters, Army Commendation Medal, Army Achievement Medal, Presidential Unit Citation (Army), National Defense Service Medal, Vietnam Service Medal, Armed Forces Expeditionary Medal, Army Service Ribbon and Overseas Service Ribbon.

After retiring from the Army, Jack worked as a Sociology professor and administrator for John Tyler Community College in Virginia until he retired in 2002. Jack started his own company in the fall of 2002 as a Workforce Development consultant and has now retired.

[Note: LTC Jack Heslin performed the duties of Liaison Officer in gathering together the five new witness statements and flight tape transcript necessary for a "Medal of Honor" recommendation from the helicopter pilots.

FORREST B. SNYDER, JR.

Forrest Snyder was born in 1945 and grew up on a tobacco farm near Damascus, Maryland, where he graduated from Damascus High School in 1963. After completing a four-year apprenticeship in the machine shop at the National Bureau of Standards, he attended Middle Tennessee State University where he graduated in 1970 with a BS in Physics, a commission as a Second Lieutenant of Field Artillery, and the promise of Helicopter Flight School.

Forrest earned the wings of an Army Aviator and transitioned into the AH-1G Huey Cobra prior to deployment to Vietnam in December 1971. Assigned to the 361st Aerial Weapons Company in Pleiku, Snyder flew in support of South Vietnamese forces during the Battle of Kontum, participating in actions at Tan Canh, Polei Kleng, Ben Het, Firebase Delta, Firebase Charlie, and Kontum City before being wounded in action.

After a lengthy recovery, he remained in the Army, serving in both Aviation and Field Artillery positions prior to leaving active duty in 1982.

Forrest holds the Vietnamese Cross of Gallantry, Army Commendation Medal, Purple Heart, Bronze Star, Air Medal with "V" device for Valor, and eleven awards of the Air Medal, the Meritorious Service Medal and the Distinguished Flying Cross.

Forrest recently retired after 31 years as a Systems Engineer by the MITRE Corporation. He and his wife, Paula, live in Sterling, Virginia.

LTC JAMES M. ("Mike") GIBBS

James M. ("Mike") Gibbs began his career as an enlisted man in the 82nd Airborne Division as an artilleryman. He attended NCO Academy in 1962 while stationed in Germany and was recognized as the top graduate. He also was awarded the General Patton Award for overall excellence.

He completed Artillery Officer Candidate School at Fort Sill, Oklahoma and after an artillery assignment there, he was selected to attend Fixed Wing Aviator training. Upon graduation, he was selected for transition into the Army's U1A (Otter) program and his first tour in Vietnam was in 1965 with the 18th Aviation Company.

On completion of his tour, he attended Helicopter Aviator training enroute to assignment with the 24th Infantry Division artillery in Germany. In 1968, he returned to Vietnam for his second tour. Mike was assigned to Company "B", 123rd Aviation Battalion as a gun section leader and then as Executive Officer.

On completion of his tour, he attended the Field Artillery Officers Advance course at Fort Sill. In conjunction with his tour there, he earned a Bachelor of Science degree in Business.

In 1971, now Major Gibbs returned to Vietnam for his third combat tour. Mike commanded Troop H (air), 17th Armored Cavalry Squadron during the "Battle for Charlie." While tasked with another mission, he requested permission to provide assistance in the rescue and pickup of the paratroopers after their call for "Help!" He was the last ship in and rescued the surrounded command group. His aircraft was targeted and under intense fire. He disregarded enemy fire and held steady, picking up the last survivors of the unit. One of the rescued officers was hit climbing aboard and his Crew Chief was shot and died. Major Gibbs was awarded the Silver Star, which is this nation's third highest award for gallantry in action.

Mike returned to Fort Sill, commanded the 17th Aviation Company (18 CH 47 aircraft). He later served as Assistant Inspector General at Fort Sill.

Major Gibbs was selected for Command and General Staff College and upon completion, served as Executive Officer of the Cleveland District Recruiting Command of Ohio. Subsequent assignments were: Deputy Aviation Officer for V Corps in Germany, Executive Officer of the Field Artillery School Brigade at Fort Sill; Director of Personnel Administration. 20th Support Group in Taegu, Korea, and his final assignment as VP Test and Experimentation Command, Fort Sill.

Among the numerous awards LTC Gibbs has received are the Silver Star, Distinguished Flying Cross, Bronze Star with one Oak Leaf cluster, Air Medal with "Valor" device, Air Medal, 43rd Award, Legion of Merit, Meritorious Service Medal with two Oak Leaf clusters, Army Commendation Medal, Army Good Conduct medal, NDSM, VSM, NOPD, Senior Parachutist Badge, Master Aviator Badge.

Upon retirement, Mike attended school for two years to become a registered radiologic technologist (X-ray technician). He worked full time in that profession at a hospital in Lawton, Oklahoma for ten years, and continues to work there part-time as needed. Mike and his wife enjoy traveling in their RV when not working and still have their home in Lawton.

Author's note: I was particularly impressed that LTC "Mike" Gibbs had flown over 1,000 combat missions. Each "Air Medal" represents 25 combat missions. Mike had 43 Air Medals, each representing 25 combat missions.

NAM NHAT PHAN

I.   Born September 9, 1943 in Hue, Central Vietnam.

II.   National Academy Military (18th Class - Nov 23 1961- 1963) Đalat, South Vietnam.

•1963-1970: Platoon Leader, Company Commander, S3 Officer (Tactical Operation - Section 3) in ARVN Airborne Division. Saigon, South Vietnam.

•1970–1973: T.O.C Officer (Tactical Operation Center) in Phước Tuy and Long An Province Headwater, South Vietnam.

•1973-1975: Secretary of Joint Military Committee 4 and 2 Party Chief Delegate Conference.

Operation Officer in POW Department. Saigon, South Vietnam. Scheduled and applied the POWs releasing and receiving plan for Vietnamese prisoners (both sides of Vietnam) and American prisoners.
•1975-1989: Detained in concentration camps in South and North Vietnam.

•1989-1993: Restricted living location in South Vietnam.

•1994-2014: Resettled in USA, having presented many lectures and book tours around the world; USA, Democracy and Freedom presentations relating my vivid experiences and the ongoing struggles for all Vietnamese people.

●**1998-2001: Social Worker at Vietnamese Social Services in Minnesota.**
●**2000-2003: University of Minnesota.**
III. Description of writing activities:

●**1968-1975:Worked within the network of the largest monthly, weekly magazine and daily news in Saigon, South Vietnam: Doi (Life), Dieu Hau (Eagle), Song (Existence), Dai Dan Toc (Great People), Doc Lap (Independence), and Song Than (Holy Wage)**

●**Participated with Saigon Radio, ARVN Radio. South Vietnam.**

●**Collaborated with SangTao (Creationist), ĐaiNga (Great Karma), HienĐai (Modern Time), and SongMoi (New Life) Publisher, Saigon, South Vietnam.**

●**1994-2014: In process of collaborating with most of the Vietnamese mass media agencies in USA, Australia, Canada, and Europe.**

IV. List of books by title or publications in which my writing has appeared:

1968-1975 in Saigon, South ViệtNam

Trace of War (Dau Binh Lua), ĐaiNga (Great Karma), Publisher (1969); Re-edited by HienĐai (Modern Time) Publisher (1973);
Along the Road No One (Doc Duong So I), ÑaiNga Publisher, (1970);
The Gate of Life on Earth (Ai Tran Gian), ĐaiNga Publisher, (1971);

Back to Death (Dua Lung Noi Chet), ĐaiNga Publisher, 1972; Re-edited by HienĐai, Publisher (1973);

Summer of Red-hot Gunfire (Mua He Đo Lua), SangTao Publisher, (1972); Re-edited by HienĐai, Publisher, (1973, 1974);

Peace and Prisoner of War (TuBinh va HoaBinh), HienĐai, Publisher (1974);

1988-2014 in USA, Australia, France

Peace and Prisoner of War (English Copy), Kháng Chiến Publisher, San Jose, CA (1988).

Tales Should Be Told (Nhung Chuyen Can Đuoc Ke Lai), Auto edition, TX (1995); Co-edition in Australia, (1996); Re-edited by Publisher, CA (1997).

Along the Farthest Way (Đuong Truong Xa Xam), Auto edition, TX (1995); Co-edition in Australia, (1996); Re-edited by Tu Quynh Publisher, CA (1997).

In Voiceless Eternal Nights (Đêm Tận Thất Thanh), Auto edition, TX (1997).

Keep Fire in Winter (Mua Đong Giu Lua), Auto edition, TX (1997); Re-edited by Tu Quynh Publisher, CA (1998).

Summer in Europe with Phan Nhat Nam (Mua He Chau Au với Phan Nhat Nam), Nam Á Publisher, Paris, France (1997).

The Stories Must To Be Told, Minnesota (2002).

The Pillars For Country, (Những Cột Trụ Chống Giữ Quê Hương), CA (2005).

A VietNam War Epilogue, CA, (2012).

Stories Along the Road, (Chuyện Dọc Dường), CA (2012); Reedited (2013).

Man's Fate–Country's Destiny, (Phận Người Vận Nước). CA(2013).

John J. Duffy

Reviewed and Re-edited

Trace of War, TuQuynh Publisher, CA (1996)
Peace and Prisoner of War, Đai Nam Publisher, CA (1996)
Summer of Red-hot Gunfire (Mua He Đo Lua), CA (2005)

V. Awards or recognition given for the writing:

•War Correspondent Award issued by ARVN Warfare General Department, Saigon, South Vietnam, 1972.

•National Literature Prize issued by Vietnamese National Resistant Movement, CA, USA (1988)

VI. Political persecution to which I was subjected:

Placed in the hardest communist concentration camps for over 14 years (1975-1989) and had to endure confinement in underground jails in two phases:

(A) From Feb. 21, 1979 to Aug. 20, 1980 in Section D Camp No 5, Lam Son, Thanh Hoa North Vietnam.

(B) From Sept. 7, 1981 to May 29, 1988:

1. Sept. 7, 1981-July 27, 1982 in Section D Camp No 5, Lam Son, Thanh Hoa, North Vietnam.

2. July 27, 1982-April 17, 1986 in Section C Camp No 5, Lam Son, Thanh Hoa, North Vietnam.

3. April 17, 1982-Jan. 8, 1988 in Thanh Cam Camp, Thanh Hoa, North Vietnam.

4. Jan 8, 1982-May 29, 1988 in Ba Sao Camp, Hà Nam Ninh, North Vietnam.

5. May 29, 1988-Jan 29, 1989 in Hàm Tân Z30D Camp, South Vietnam.

CW4 DENNIS WATSON

From my earliest memories, I dreamed of becoming a pilot, but was convinced that was a lofty goal for a South Alabama farm boy. Because I was born and raised in Enterprises Alabama, I watched as airplanes and helicopters from "Camp" Rucker flew overhead. I continued to dream as I progressed through school. During my first year in Junior College in Enterprise, I made a monumental decision that would forever change my life, and joined the Army for the specific purpose of becoming a helicopter pilot.

I had been married for four months when I arrived in Vietnam on September 3, 1971 at the age of twenty and was assigned to the 192nd AHC in Dong Ba Thin. The 192nd was well over-strength. Neither the slick nor the gun platoon wanted a new "wobbly one" so since the Slick Platoon Commander had time-in-grade, he had the right to reject me and cast me to the gun platoon where I was no less welcome. Having neither gun transition nor experience, I received my first on-the-job training during my first "gunfight."

Inbound, the pilot punching off pairs of rockets, I watched the tiny lights whizz by going the other way. Still naïvely invulnerable, I thought the experience to be "way cool while the pilot was screaming, "Shoot!" He was incredulous to learn that I didn't know how a mini-gun handle was stowed overhead and pulling the pin would drop it down and awaken the hydraulically operated mini-guns. My tenure as a gun pilot got better, but not by much. The 192nd stood down in January 1972, at which time I was reassigned to 7/17

ACS. Because I spent the first four months flying guns, I was one of the few that became a slick pilot mid-tour. So, although I never became an Aircraft Commander, I was one of the finest co-pilots the Cav had ever known.

Unlike the 192nd AHC, my tour with the Cav was filled with difficult days. We were in The Battle of Kontum, which was part of a full-scale assault by the NVA on the South. Whether watching a C-130 take off from the Kontum airport, stall, then cartwheel, or crossing Dak To airport with a flight of five helicopters while being shot at with the main turrets of enemy tanks, or looking into the eyes of a valiant door gunner as he screamed "hit" and closed his eyes for the last time. All gave some; some gave all: Dallas Nihsen, Gerald Spradlin, Larry Morrow, Wayne Finch, and Charles Britt were among those killed during the spring and summer of 1972. That many losses in that short span should have told me something, but like my counterparts, I knew no better. I was fortunate to survive my tour and departed H Troop enroute to "The World" on August 9, 1972 at age 21.

I was assigned to Ft. Lewis, Washington and transitioned into the new OH-58 helicopter. Our mission was IBA, Itsy Bitsy Airlines, with an occasional assignment to fly new Artillery Officers to the impact range where they practiced directing live fire from a helicopter. Ft. Lewis was a dream job and the best flying club one could ask for. Our "Missions" ranged from lunch at the Puyallup airport, to watching whales breach in Puget Sound, or playing hide and seek in the Cascade Mountains. And there was that occasional transport mission.

My father died unexpected in 1974. He left behind a wife and four year-old son, my baby brother, who was born the day I graduated from high school. Because of him, I requested and was granted a compassionate reassignment to Ft. Rucker. At Ft. Rucker I requested to become a Contact Instructor pilot. I attended the Instrument Instructor pilot course there. Training complete, I successfully instructed entry level instrument students for three years with none ever failing a check ride. Along the way, I became an Instrument Examiner and Contact Instructor Pilot.

In 1977, I received orders for Germany with Cobra transition enroute. My previous gun experience assured me that because of my aversion to spewing death and destruction, I was not gun material. I requested a Chinook or fixed wing transition instead, but my request was denied. So, in the spring of 1977, I made a decision to separate from the Army and in the fall of 1977, became a full-time student at Auburn University.

Near the middle of my first quarter at Auburn, I received a call from a Ft. Rucker mentor, Frank Carlisle. He "told" me he would see me at Alabama National Guard drill the following weekend in Birmingham, Alabama. I assured him he would not. But he would not take "no" for an answer and made me a deal—come to the drill and if you don't like it, I won't bother you again." The rest is history. Because of Frank's call, I joined the Guard without a break in service and in 2000 I retired from the Guard with 30 years of service.

Having a wife and child made it extremely difficult to be a full-time student while taking the maximum course loads, working in the University bookstore during the week, and flying with the Alabama National

Guard on the weekends. Because I was an instrument IP/Examiner and Contact Instructor, I had the luxury of choosing additional drill opportunities based on the needs of my peers for my IP/Examiner services.

I graduated from Auburn after nine straight quarters, was offered and accepted a job with General Motors in Decatur, Alabama as an Industrial Engineer. I soon learned that my desk job did not satisfy me. During my tenure at GM, I was offered a job in Dallas, Texas flying for an oil company. A new Cessna 210 and Bell 206 awaited my arrival. I accepted the job, turned in my resignation to GM, and came home to find my wife, Sheila preparing the first closet for packing. Her cheeks were covered with tears and our small daughters were nearby without their happy faces. Sheila had made all the sacrifices required by college and the military. I reversed my career move and managed to retract my GM resignation.

Eighteen months later, in 1982, I did leave GM and went into Industrial Sales. My sales career took me to Gulf Breeze, Florida, then to Fairhope, Alabama where Sheila, my wife of 42 years, and I have lived since 1983. We have two daughters who are married, successful, and each of whom has given us two beautiful grandchildren.

Along the way I had the opportunity to pilot the EMS helicopter for the University of South Alabama from 1988 through 1996, at which time I was diagnosed with simple partial seizures (non-debilitating). The word "seizure" has no modifiers in the eyes of the FAA, so my flying career ended abruptly. I moved back into sales. I spent the last five years of my work career starting and managing a manufacturing facility in Mobile, Alabama for an Orlando, Florida company, Steel Constructions.

At age 59 I became a casualty of the economic downturn and lost my job. Fortunately, God blessed me with a way to retire instead of joining the ranks of the unemployed. I have been retired now for almost four years and still pinch myself every morning when I wake up for the sheer joy of life.

Many years ago I considered that every sunset I saw might be my last, and like many others, lived with guarded expectation that I would see the next. Many years later, I would sit at my General Motors desk amidst a myriad of other General Motors engineers and contemplate my future. I contemplated whether I would one day regret having spent my work life progressing from one desk to the next high level desk, never having left the building. I didn't want to look back on my life and wonder what could have been. So, in 1983, I made the monumental decision to step outside the walls. Because of that decision, I have experienced the excitement of knowing that every day will be different from the day before.

I have made four monumental decisions in my life. The first was to marry Sheila. The second was to pursue my dream of flying and be rewarded with all the experiences that have come from that decision. The third was to move outside the walls of a General Motors plant and enjoy all the excitement of experiencing several rewarding professional opportunities, not the least of which was my tenure as an EMS pilot. The fourth and most important, was becoming a follower of Christ in 1975. I am convinced that His influence in my life has been responsible for all the joy and excitement I have experienced and will continue to experience throughout eternity.

John J. Duffy

SECTION III

APPENDIX

**Excerpt from Tape Recording
of last rescue helicopter
15 April 1972
Pilot: Major James ("Mike") Gibbs
Co-pilot: CW4 Dennis Watson**

**Tape recording made by CW4 Watson
Later transcribed by CW4 Watson**

[Begin Excerpt]

April 15, 1972

(DC) Dusty Cyanide. John Duffy, MAJ. In charge of group to be extracted.

(MG) Number 4 Huey in flight of four. James "Mike" Gibbs, MAJ. Call sign: Embalmer six.

(DW) Dennis Watson, WO1, Embalmer six's co-pilot.

(PB33) Number 3 Huey in flight of four.

(DN) Embalmer six left seat door gunner, Dallas Nihsen.

(DG) Embalmer six right side door gunner.

(UT22) Air Mission Coordinator. Call sign: Undertaker 22. AH-1G Cobra Gunship; a.k.a. Snake/Gun.

* * * * *

(DW internal to MG) Over the ridge. He'll leave a smoke for us.

(DW) Chalk four is two miles.

(DC) Cobra, Cobra, they're 25 meters away. They're in that wood line. Go get 'em.

(DC) Cobra, Cobra, they're 25 meters away, to my sierra, to my sierra.

(UT24) Roger, Dusty. We're inbound. Keep your heads down...(sound of 24's minigun firing.)

(PB33) 33's out, breaking right.

(DW) Chalk's four's a mile.

(DC) Cobra, Cobra, they're 25 meters to my sierra.

(DW) I know they're down there.

(DC) Over the woodline. Get it down. All the way, all the way down.

(MG internal to DW) Just coming out...

(DW internal to MG) There go the gunships. Beautiful...beautiful.

(DC) Good show Cobras.

(DW) And chalk four's short final.

(MG internal to DW) Do you have the people?

(DW internal to MG) G...D...that was close.

(MG internal to DW) I don't have any people.

(DW internal to MG) I don't either but if they down here we'll get 'em.

(MG) OK we need some guidance. Where's the people?

(DW internal to MG) They're over here.

(PB33) Dusty, Undertaker 22. Where do you want these people taken?

(DG & DN internal) Taking fire...

(DW internal to crew) I think we're taking fire. We're taking fire.

(DW) Chalk four's taking fire. Be making a go around.

(DW internal to MG) Sir, if I didn't see B-40's I'll kiss your ass.

(MG internal to DB and DN) Ok, hold your fire.

(DW internal to MG) OK, if I didn't see B-40's sir I will kiss your ass.

(DG internal to crew) I got a round stuck...2 rounds stuck in my barrel.

(PB Lead) We took fire just about due east of that LZ.

(MG internal to DW) Ok, let's come right.

(DW internal to MG) You got it, sir. OK.

(PB33) Six, you think you can get back in there?

(MG) That's affirmative. I couldn't see the people that time. I don't think we had a smoke left from number three.

(DC) *unintelligible, something about woodline.*

(DW internal to DG and DN) Did you see any people?

(DG internal to DG) Yea, I sure did.

((UT22) Dusty, are they still down there in that same woodline?

(DC) Yes we are but just one gun.

(UT22) Dusty you still on the LZ or moving away from it?

(DC) We're moving to the whiskey...er...to the November echo.

(UT22) Roger, I'll be in with 20 mm.

(DG internal) There go bad guy right there, right there, on that trail.

(MG internal) There's a what?

(DB internal) There's bad guys carrying rockets back there.

(DW) OK, Undertaker, we got people all along these trails our {sic} here, out your 9 er 3 o'clock.

(MG) Whole bunches of 'em.

(DG) I ain't gonna be able to shoot this gun no more.

(UT24) Unless you draw fire don't engage.

(MG internal) OK, do you know where the friendlies are?

(PB33) OK, 22, this load of people I got on board I'll be taking them into Tan Can and coming back out if you need any help.

(DW internal) I really didn't see any people.

(UT22) Dusty, Undertaker 22, how was that?

(UT22) Dusty, Undertaker 22.

(DC) Garbled radio.

(UT22) OK. We shot the area up. I'll bring in my slick and we'll see what happens.

(DC) Still got small arms. We've moved about 25 meters. We're gonna stop here. We got five people left. Over.

(UT22) Roger.

(MG) 22 this is six. I'm on a supposed final. I don't really know where the people are.

(MG) 22, you got me?

(Mg internal) I'm right under one of them.

(MG internal) OK, watch for the people.

(DC) On target...On target.

(DB internal) My 60 doesn't work.

(MG internal) OK

(DW internal) OK, that's the LZ up there. Where the people are I don't know.

(DC) Still got small arms fire. Still got small arms fire. Automatic rifles.

(MG internal) We got yellow smoke over there.

(MG) 22 we got yellow smoke way to the north over there.

(UT24) OK, if you hang a left, turn left one-eighty, six.

(MG) Left one-eighty.

(U24) Still drawing small arms fire from the tree line down here. Ok now turn right. Right 90.

(MG internal) OK, I see where they are.

(UT24) Right 90. Across the tree at your 12 are the friendlies and bad guys are in the trees.

(DW internal) Right here's the people...here they are.

(MG internal) You see 'em?

(DW internal) Right, got 'em in sight.

(DG internal) Right there

(UT24) Bad guys at your left. Friendlies at your eleven.

(UT24) 24 is on your left.

(MG internal) OK, I got friendlies off on the left here too.

(DC) Ease down.

(DG Internal) We're taking incoming over here.

(MG internal) That's rockets.

(DW internal) Snakes

(Mg internal) OK, I got friends American type, coming down.

(DN internal) Clear down left

(MG internal) Watch the blades.

(DW internal) OK, sir, you're clear down over here. Just kind of hold it down and let them crawl on. It's gonna be real rough.

(DW internal) I'll monitor the gages{sic}

(MG internal) Still on the controls.

Crack of first round through the cockpit.

(MG internal) Still on the controls.

Crack of second round through cockpit. I believe this is the round which struck Dallas Nihsen. Penetrated right front just above windshield, missed my head by about a foot, traveled diagonally to left side of aircraft, through transmission well and struck Dallas in the back.

(DN internal) Hey, Hey, hit!

(MG internal) We're taking fire.

(DN internal) Hey, hit.

(MG internal) Still on the controls

(DW internal) He's hit. Nihsen's hit, sir! Sir, Nihsen's hit! Nihsen's hit!

(DW internal) OK, I got it. We got one hit. We got one hit.

(DG Internal) Go! Go! Go! Go!

(DW internal) Go, Sir.

(DG internal) Get outta here!

(MG internal) OK, we're coming out.

(DW internal) Roger, you're good, you're good...you're good.

(MG internal) We're coming out. We got one wounded on the left.

(DW internal) You're OK

(MG internal) we got everybody on?

(DG internal) Everybody's here.

(DG internal) Go ahead, go ahead.

(DW internal) Go, sir. 40 lbs of torque, lookin' good. Don't know if we're hit. Gages {sic} are green.
(MG internal) Comin' up over the ridge.

(UT24) OK, I got people moving in the grass but it looks like friendlies.

(MG internal) We're taking fire.

(DW internal) OK, sir, we're looking good.

(MG internal) Are the gages {sic} OK?

(DW internal) You're {sic} gages {sic} are OK. You're 40 lbs of torque. Everything's green.

(MG internal) Check Nihsen.

(DW) Sir, he's moving. He's OK.

(MG internal) Hey, get Nihsen in. (*Slumped over toward outside of aircraft, restricted by seat belt.*)

(DW internal) He's strapped in, sir, he can't go anywhere.

(MG) OK, we got the man on the left (Interrupted)

(DG internal) Get some altitude. My gun is jammed up again.

(UT24) Did you get our Uniform Sierra man?

(MG) That's affirm. We got the Uniform Sierra and my Uniform Sierra on the left side is hit.

(DG internal to someone in back) You OK!?

(UT24) OK. Well, let's not just shoot at 'em unless we can draw some fire.

(MG) OK. We're off and we got the Uniform Sierra off the ground and we got the man (DC-John Duffy) working on the guy in the left seat. My code name Nihsen's hit.

(UT24) Rog.

(MG) OK, give me a count of how many people we got.

(Pallbearer 33) 24, understand they got all the people outta there?

(UT24) We got the American and there's people running all over down here.

(DW internal) He (Duffy) says he'll be ok if you get him the F..k outta here. Let's go.

(DW internal) Hospital, sir.

(MG internal) Kontum?

(DW internal) Kontum...hospital.

[End excerpt]

[Note: The Crew Chief, Dallas Nihsen was hanging by his tether harness from the aircraft. Major Duffy retrieved him, covered the entrance wound to his chest and was treating the exit wound when he died in Major Duffy's arms before arriving at the hospital.]

The Battle for "Charlie"

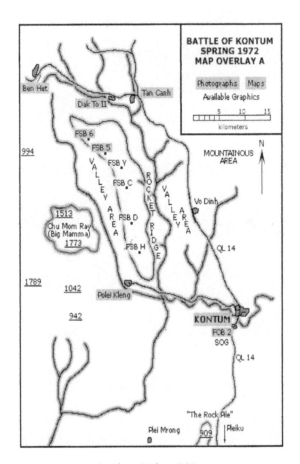

Rocket Ridge FSBs:
Y (Yankee), C (Charlie)
D (Delta), H (Hotel)
[http://www.armchairgeneral.com/
forums/showthread.php?t=110283]

FSB C on map is the pass being blocked, designated "Charlie." The 11th Vietnamese Airborne Battalion held back the elite NVA 320th Division ("Steel" or "Dien Bien" Division), reinforced by the NVA 66th Regiment of the NVA 3rd Division for two weeks, disrupting their timetable.

John J. Duffy

ABOUT THE AUTHOR

John J. Duffy, the poet, has published five poetry books and previously been nominated for the Pulitzer Prize in poetry. *Warman*, *Peaceman*, and *Sageman* document his war experience as a Special Forces Commander. His *The Bush Chronicles* gives a rendition of the most important events in George W. Bush's first term as President.

John served as a Commander in Special Operations and is a highly decorated officer. He rose from Sergeant to Major and has sixty plus awards and decoration, including the Distinguished Service Cross and eight Purple Hearts.

After military service, John held senior positions in Publishing and Finance. He founded an investment firm which was sold to Ameritrade.

"Chromosome 23" was published in 2013 and nominated for a Pulitzer Prize. It's a story about you, me, and all of us, before and future, and delves into the "soup mix" of life. The focus is on the "XX" (female) and the "XY" (male) chromosome.

John is retired in Santa Cruz, California and writes poetry. Two of his poems are inscribed on a monument dedicated to Forward Air Controllers in Colorado Springs, Colorado.

John J. Duffy

CPSIA information can be obtained
at www.ICGtesting.com
Printed in the USA
LVHW021740150722
723529LV00005B/317

9 781499 683615